3

MW00450349

PAINT AND PAPER

PAINT AND PAPER

IN DECORATION

DAVID OLIVER

RIZZOLI
NEW YORK

Author's note: Please do not rely on page representation for colour accuracy.
To view final paint colour, it is recommended that you purchase a sample pot
or colour chart. Please visit www.paintlibrary.co.uk for a list of suppliers.

First published in the United States of America in 2007 by
Rizzoli International Publications, Inc.
300 Park Avenue South
New York, NY 10010
www.rizzoliusa.com

Originally published in the United Kingdom in 2007 by
Conran Octopus Limited, a part of Octopus Publishing Group
a Hachette Livre UK Company
2–4 Heron Quays, London E14 4JP
www.conran-octopus.co.uk

Publishing director Lorraine Dickey
Editor Sybella Marlow
Copy editor Alison Wormleighton

Art director Jonathan Christie
Designer Lucy Gowans
Picture researcher Emily Hedges

Production manager Angela Young

2007 2008 2009 2010 / 10 9 8 7 6 5 4 3 2 1
ISBN: 978-0-8478-3018-3
Library of Congress Control Number: 2007924728

Printed in China

CONTENTS

INTRODUCTION

INTRODUCTION

Colour is all around us and we often do not even notice it, but our reaction to it is wholly instinctive. A colour scheme is such a personal choice that I will not attempt to tell you which shades to choose. Instead, I'll guide you through the process of overcoming the modern phenomenon I call paint analysis paralysis. Although paint is probably the cheapest part of the grand redecoration process, it is one of the hardest choices to make and can go horribly wrong. It is difficult to make the leap from a small paint swatch to a whole room or even an entire home. Consequently, many of the clients I meet have a fear of using colour themselves. In this book I want to reveal how enjoyable the process can be, remove your reservations about it and redirect your energies so you can create a scheme that reflects the character of your home as well as your own personality.

Colour is fundamental to every aspect of your life, and subconsciously it is probably the driving force behind much of your decision-making. The eye is attracted to colour before we see an object itself, which means that colour has an immediate effect, both physically and emotionally. It is necessary to understand the effect colour has on mood before you leap straight in and decide to use a particular colour throughout your scheme. Not only is experimenting with colour fun, it helps you find solutions and even new colours you hadn't thought were appealing.

Colour has no absolutes. Throughout the ages, paint manufacturers have produced complex charts, which have proved confusing and which have been driven mainly by the constraints of historical styles and architectural features. When I first attempted to decorate my home, I found there was a multitude of choices but not one range that really epitomized what I was looking for. I therefore decided to create a range of colours that I felt were a cross-section of traditional and contemporary and were visually appetizing, diverse and adaptable to how we like to live today. I began to create a palette that reflected both my mood and current trends.

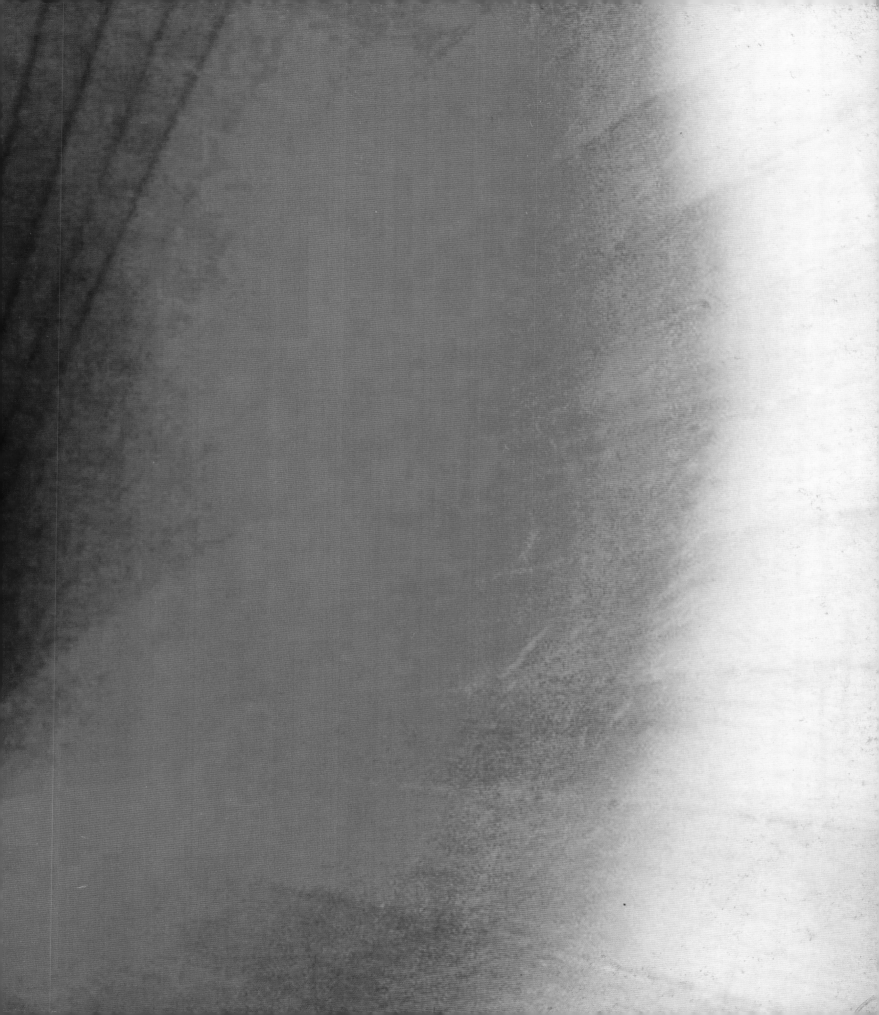

Learning to interpret colour is the clearest way to find a solution. Hopefully this book will influence and inspire you to formulate the best scheme for your home, whether now or in the future. By using the techniques explained in the following chapters, you will avoid making expensive mistakes and will be able to embrace colour, pattern and light. Colours cannot be viewed in isolation, and using variations of the three key types of palette – monochromatic, analogous and contrasting – for different architectural styles will produce a successful result.

Monochromatic palettes are possibly the easiest to use, as essentially you are using one colour with a varying degree of tones or shades. My Architectural Colours range of paints, available at Paint & Paper Library, is perfect for this approach. It consists of a range of 24 colours with 5 tonal variations to allow you to use a colour-by-number system to paint different areas, such as the walls, ceiling, cornicing (coves), skirting (baseboards) and other woodwork. The analogous colour palette is accessible and multifunctional – though it requires research, it produces a fantastic effect. My Original Colours range provides a great way to find out which colours work best together for this type of scheme. Contrasting colour palettes are more personal, more experimental and a braver direction to explore. However, the end result can be outstanding.

I am convinced that the hand and eye are drawn to surfaces where they have rested before: areas seasoned by the weather or worn by constant use can have beautiful textures and soft, mellow colours that are highly inspirational. Strong sunlight can also affect the natural oxides in paint, so over time they slowly fade into other fantastic shades. Light is important in the way colour is used, as it can change the way you perceive a pigment.

When devising colour schemes you have to start somewhere, and so in this book I will guide you from your departure point to your arrival at a new scheme. However, finding your starting point is difficult, because colour is everywhere and you have a wealth of choice. Accept it as a very human luxury – many animals only see in tones of black and white – and one with which we have many strong, meaningful associations through culture, experience and daily life. Surprisingly, it is often the most obvious combinations that will work best. Inspiring colours and palettes are all around you, so your ideal palettes may be right under your nose.

Don't be a slave to fashion or historical style – trust your own judgement, because the beauty of colour is in the eye of the beholder. Combining personal choices, a few basic colour theories and a good knowledge of your home and its character will undoubtedly lead to a successful scheme. Decorating is expressive, so, just as you would when choosing something to wear, see the language of colour as an opportunity to make a statement.

INSPIRATION

You can find inspiration for colours in the simplest everyday objects, such as the faded buff and ochre tones on the wood from this building.

"Chance favours only the prepared mind" LOUIS PASTEUR

This quote regularly resounds through my mind when I am preparing a new project. Choosing colours can be one of the most enjoyable aspects of decorating a home, but the inspiration for the colours should not be left to chance. Creating a workable plan is the best approach to the process of choosing colour palettes, and in this book I will show you how I go about it.

Colour choice should be based on personal taste and instinct. Rather like cooking, it reflects your personality and is open to individual interpretation, free from stifling conventions and prescriptive styles. There are no rights and wrongs – what is subtle to one person is insipid to another; one person's "cheerful" is another's "garish".

Before you start to plan your palette, however, it is vital to undertake research on various levels, in order to establish what you need and also what you actually like. If you are impatient to get on with the more creative part, just remember that this approach is wholly beneficial to the end result. It will ensure that the colours you use will suit your home and your lifestyle as well as your personality. In addition, it will enable you to create the most indispensable tool for planning your scheme – the mood board (see page 52), which channels your creativity, gives direction and, most importantly, visualizes the mood of the environment.

CRUCIAL FACTORS

The first step in the process is to assess what factors will affect the scheme. This is the point at which you realize just how many components are involved. The initial and obvious question is – is the project an isolated room, a hallway, a number of rooms, or the whole home? Following on from this is the question of whether the home requires a unified scheme with no abrupt colour changes or whether each room is to have a different and individual impact. Once you have answered these questions, you will have a better idea as to where you are going and the scale of the project, and you can consider the properties of each room to be decorated.

NATURAL LIGHT

The most important of these is the amount of natural light the room receives, which dramatically affects the way colours look and determines what colours can be used there (see page 55). Daylight is itself extremely variable. Because the natural light in a room is always changing, not just through the year but also hour by hour, you need to observe the effect it has on the room throughout the day.

In temperate climates, the light is quite cold, which often makes colours look dull. The direction a room faces also has an effect on this – in the northern hemisphere, north-facing rooms do not get a lot of sun, while south-facing rooms are sun-drenched. The size of the windows and what is outside the windows (buildings? trees? sky?) are other factors affecting the amount of light coming into a room. Find out which way your room faces and monitor how the light changes throughout the day. Remember that this will vary according to season. The time of day when you will use the room comes into the equation, too. For example, it might not matter that the room is dark if it is to be used only at night and in the early morning.

Right: Natural light can change constantly but can also be made to change according to the building materials you choose to direct, absorb or reflect the prevailing conditions. These beautiful large wooden planks create a dramatic rhythmic light screen in a raw urban hallway.

ARCHITECTURAL ASPECTS

How you treat the architectural elements of the room is another key aspect of planning a colour scheme. This is particularly important if they are attractive features such as plasterwork, woodcarving or a fire surround (fireplace mantel) to which you would like to call attention, or awkward features you would prefer to camouflage. For my Architectural Colours range (see pages 144–167), I have devised a tonal colour-by-number system for ceilings, cornices (coves), walls and woodwork. These chromatically arranged colour palettes enable you to create a harmonious balance of colour and light by accentuating or complementing all of these elements.

The size and shape of a room have to be taken into account, too. For example, smaller rooms with high ceilings can only look resolved when the ceiling is painted in a related or chromatic colour (see page 122) to the wall scheme. This makes the disproportionate scale or height of the room less noticeable than if painted in a contrasting white.

ROOM FUNCTION

Another factor to consider is the function of the room. Nearly every room has a different purpose, and in order to ascertain your precise requirements you may need to spend time thinking about how you use it.

These days the kitchen is generally the hub of the home and as a result often includes an eating area and perhaps also a seating area with sofas, creating a family room. Or it may be open-plan together with the living room, dining room or family room. However it is arranged, the kitchen is one of the warmest rooms in the home, which will affect the scheme. Kitchens, with their cabinets, work surfaces and appliances, often have the greatest mix of materials, and the whole gamut of finishes, from matt to high gloss. I find therefore that kitchens often require only two or three interior colours at most – any more than this and they would look overcrowded and confused. The same applies to utility or laundry rooms and pantries.

Reception rooms such as living, drawing, or sitting rooms are a different story. These are where you can be experimental, daring and have fun creating the maximum impact in order to impress. The colour of a room is usually the first thing a visitor notices and is often the main point of reference when a person is asked to describe the mood. I believe that the most successful designs have the same sort of serendipity as a break in the clouds or that magic moment when the breeze drops. Like most rooms, reception rooms have dual purposes, at opposite ends of the scale. We all want to live and spend time in a comfortable place where we can enjoy the pleasures of an exiled morning or a measured afternoon. At the same time, we want the room to be smart and welcoming to visitors.

With the right choice of colour palette, reception rooms can offer all of this.

The buoyant social function of a dining room, or a separate dining area in an open-plan room, means that it can take on a variety of moods – ranging from Sunday lunches and evenings at home with friends to formal dinners and annual family gatherings. The right colour scheme will cater for these changing moods and times of day, whether clean and fresh for daytime meals or subtle and romantic for evening entertaining. Underpinning this is the fact that most dining rooms, and many dining areas, are symmetrical, owing to the large, central table. This room therefore requires tranquillity and balance combined with subtle energy.

Opposite left: The colour scheme of a room can be derived from the objects that it houses; the soft porcelain china contrasted with rough logs are the departure point for this scheme.
Above: Exotic collections and simple patterns can transform a room into a delightful sanctuary for pleasure, memory and style.

Opposite right: In kitchens think about what core colour would tie together all the appliances we have on display making the function the focal point rather than the empty fields of wall. Don't be afraid to go dark on the wall and ceiling in small utility areas to unify the overall space.

Bedrooms are havens of comfort and relaxation, private retreats where an atmosphere of calm should prevail. Many, however, serve a dual function, such as a study or children's playroom, in which case the atmosphere may be not so much sybaritic as fresh and bright. Bathrooms, too, can be sensory oases or crisp and simple, depending on who will be using them. Like kitchens, they often encompass a plethora of materials, surfaces and textures, from marble or limestone to glass, acrylic or porcelain. They are also usually the smallest rooms in the home, so aim to use no more than two or three different colours. If the bathroom is off the bedroom, you may wish for the colours of the two rooms to be linked to create a seemless flow.

Colour palettes are often overlooked in hallways, but even when it is small a hallway offers the first impression of your home. In addition, it unifies your decorating plan, linking rooms designed in isolation. What is more, because everyone is simply passing through a hallway, the colours can be more adventurous than you might want to use in a room where you spend a lot of time.

Above: Link adjacent bathrooms with the colour cousins of the main bedroom. The colours here lead easily from one room to the next as if one was a shadow of the other.

Opposite: Favourite collections can be a lovely way to decorate a second home in an easy to understand, unfussy, low maintainance kind of way. These simple multi-coloured tiles form a sweet embellishment for a Mediterranean rendered bed head (headboard).

Opposite: A treasured object or possession can be the starting point for any colourful scheme. Here the colours of the Indian painting could be carried onto fabrics or wallpaper.

Above: Variety in repetition is a charming way to play with the different architectural elements of a room. Steps painted in alternative colours create a melody of colour like a child's xylophone.

STYLE

Yet another factor that will affect your colour choice is style, since certain colours, or colour combinations, are often associated with particular styles, such as white with modernism and earth colours with the country look. Identify whether there are any strong design styles or influences that you covet or that already feature in your furnishings – from rustic to contemporary, urban to ethnic, minimalist to opulent. When researching in the next stage you can take all these characteristics into account.

SOURCES OF INSPIRATION

A sense of colour and composition is instinctive, but knowing how to translate your preferences into a cohesive scheme is less automatic. Therefore, the next, and most creative, step is actually to seek inspiration for the colours you will want to use. There are no strict rules for how to go about this, but once you are on the right track you will have moments of self-awareness that give you an insight into how you would like to live and what to aim for. From the infinite world of colour around you, you can choose those hues that resonate with you and will allow you to create a home environment reflecting your personal preferences. You may be surprised how simple it can be to bring your own individual style to your home.

It is the colours you are most attracted to that will be the most satisfying to live with, so look around you – with which colours do you instinctively feel most comfortable? Which ones put you in a good mood? Do you have a strong emotional response to any? Try to analyse what it is you like (or dislike) about them – their depth, purity, softness, warmth or whatever. Search through books and magazines and identify the colours to which you are drawn. If you collect these pictures together, you will probably start to see a pattern emerging, whether it is a preference for bright, saturated colour, soft pastels, smoky shades or muted neutrals.

Above: Packaging is a good place to look for inspiration. A simple red black faded paper greige LP record cover is a lovely combination of colours with which to start.
Opposite above and below: Existing possessions are a great place to start to explore how you might like to redecorate. Squirrelling away in forgotten basements and store rooms can unfurl all kinds of forgotten ideas.

POSSESSIONS

Clothing, jewellery, furniture, objets d'art, paintings and other possessions, many of which are related to your interests and influences, may be an excellent source of inspiration. Think about the colours you like to wear, for example. Clothing is a form of self-expression, representing what you like to cloak yourself in, how you see yourself and how you wish to present yourself to the world. In fact, the link between fashion textiles and home furnishings has become much closer in recent years. Your jewellery preferences can also guide you. Not only do metallic colours suggest a more extravagant design scheme but the hues of gems and precious stones are often exquisite. Your preferences in these metals and gemstones will give you a useful insight into colours you might love in your home.

Aside from their value in revealing your subconscious colour preferences, your possessions, such as favourite objets d'art or furnishings, however small, may provide a starting point for your decorating palette. I have found in the past with my own houses that a particular lamp base or beautiful desk has triggered off a whole scheme.

Unless you are starting completely from scratch, you will probably need to incorporate some existing furniture and furnishings. It is vital to consider the items that will not be painted or changed, such as upholstered furniture, curtains, carpets and floors. In fact, you could make a virtue of necessity and let these serve as the basis of your palette. It's obviously false economy to let these dictate a whole scheme if you don't actually like the colours, but if you do they can be quite useful in reducing the vast array of choices to a manageable range of colour choices.

Collections of glass or ceramics, such as Wedgwood, Midwinter Pottery, Majolica or Bristol Blue, for example, are fabulous sources of inspiration. I have found that my own collections have a diverse yet generic palette based on colours seen in the wonderful Italian cities of Urbino, Rome, Bologna and Milan, where influential artists such as Raphael and Bramante worked. The strong cobalt blue representing glittering skies in Renaissance frescoes, alongside leafy greens and subtle yellow ochres, have provided extensive colour combinations for many a client's house.

Opposite: Colours from far away places can be replicated on your return through regional purchases or from paint finishes copied from techniques used far afield.

INFLUENCES ON MY OWN PALETTE

Inspiration is obviously completely idiosyncratic, but I have found that the major influences on my own colour palette fall into four categories: historical architecture and design; the world of art and, to a lesser extent, cinema; nature; and everyday consumer products. These four areas cover a wealth of inspiration, colour combinations and departure points for a variety of schemes. By looking at these influences, you will be able to see how I developed my Architectural Colours and Original Colours (see from pages 71 and 145), and how similar sources of inspiration could work for you. You will also discover my personal favourites.

THE WORLD OF ART AND CINEMA

Five expressive yet diverse artists – Josef Albers, Mark Rothko, Yves Klein, Giorgio Morandi and Anish Kapoor – have had a significant influence on my approach. All are masters of colour. It is their distinctive use of it that draws me to their work and engages the viewer.

Josef Albers is...

Notable for his work on the juxtaposition of colour, the German-born US painter Josef Albers (1888–1976) has taught me about the often dramatic effects that colour combinations have on hue and tone. All colour selection involves a personal response, as Albers splendidly explained: "As 'gentlemen prefer blondes,' so everyone has a preference for certain colours and prejudices against others. This applies to colour combinations as well."

In his book *Interaction of Color* Albers expanded on the way colours are used and perceived in every level of art, architecture, textiles, graphics and interior design. With his long, experimental series of paintings based on one design and sharing the title Homage to the Square, he treated paintings as "platters of colour." Exploring the illusion in which the central square, lying between the inner and outer squares, subtly takes on the hue of its neighbours, Albers affirmed that colour has many faces and that one colour can appear as two different colours.

From Josef Albers's teachings, I learned how powerfully changeable colour can be, depending on the light and the surrounding colours. I regularly refer to *Interaction of Color* when making final decisions about a scheme, and I believe that my outlook on the use of colour is similar to that of Albers, who said: "Colour is like cooking. The cook puts in more or less salt, that's the difference!"

Opposite: Inspiration can be found in the most unlikely of everyday places. I love discovering new colour combinations in unappreciated and often neglected objects, building or places.

Above: "Homage to Square": Terra Caliente by Josef Albers. Abers explored how a colour that appears to operate cohesively next to another colour on one surface can surprisingly operate completely differently on another surface or in different light conditions.

Mark Rothko is...
The Russian-born US painter Mark Rothko (1903-70) has also had a big influence on my outlook. By sitting in the Rothko room at London's Tate Modern art gallery, I pursue a personal meditative process and acknowledge the splendour of his transgressive colour.

Rothko had a very sensitive approach to colour. He reaffirmed the notion that there is more to it than the mere visual beauty of colour relationships, musing that it is "merely an instrument" to communicate basic human emotion: "The fact that people break down and cry when confronted with my pictures shows that I can communicate those basic human emotions... the people who weep before my pictures are having the same religious experience I had when painting them. And if you say you are moved only by their colour relationships then you miss the point."

Nevertheless, defying Rothko's admonitions, I do also rely on the visual allure of his colour blends, finding their bewitching intensity an arousing and spiritual experience. He was fascinated by the secrets of Pompeii (see page 42), and his colours have regularly been compared to those in the wall paintings discovered in the excavations there. Rothko's large, sombre paintings contain evocative often related colours such as blood red and burnt umber, griege and lamp blacks, or fiery rust and solar yellows.

Yves Klein is...
Like my Australian self, the French painter Yves Klein (1928-62) was always drawn to the limitless blue expanses of sea and sky that dominated his life on the sunny Mediterranean coast. Interestingly, through meditative processes, Klein searched for the colours that best conveyed the concepts he was striving to communicate through his art. One of these processes, which directly relates to rooms with little light, was his work in a basement. To mask the claustrophobic quality of the windowless room, Klein created a false sky by painting the ceiling blue. This marked the first time he created a monochromatic painted surface using the colour that symbolized limitless space and spiritual purity for him.

Embarking on a series of monochromatic works, Klein patented the colour IKB (International Klein Blue), a deep ultramarine blue that became his trademark. A great influence on the Minimalist movement, he was heralded as an innovator, for not only having invented his own colour but for having used it for self-promotion. His first exhibition featured monochrome canvases of identical size, shape and hue – the only difference was the price.

Klein explained his own attitude towards colours as follows: "For me, each nuance of a colour is in some way an individual, a being who is not only from the same race as the base colour, but who definitely possesses a distinct character and personal soul."

Intensities of colour fascinate me, particularly the fact that they can have such an effect on an environment. This theory led me to establish my Architectural Colours paint range which enables you to create a harmonious balance of colour and light by accentuating or complementing the various architectural elements of your room.

Giorgio Morandi is...
An artist who has had a profound effect on my paint analysis is the Italian painter Giorgio Morandi (1890-1964), whom I regard as a master of colour and technique. Morandi's sensitivity to colour, tone and compositional balance is undeniably impressive. He was also inspired by elements of nature and by everyday objects, as he explained: "What interests me the most is expressing what's in nature, in the invisible world, that is."

Morandi had the ability to shift moods by setting exquisitely adjusted, muted, nameless hues side by side. He worked with a limited palette of greyed and pearly tones, which often remind me of the colours seen in rock and mineral formations, another great source of inspiration. For me, the delicacy of tone and subtlety of design of his still lifes present a calm and soothing inspiration for any room in the house.

Above: "Untitled" by Mark Rothko.

Anish Kapoor is...

Through his blurring of the boundaries between painting and sculpture as well as his use of intense colour, the Indian-born artist Anish Kapoor (b. 1954) has been a huge source of inspiration for my work. In a similar style to that of Yves Klein, Kapoor's art often comprises simple, curved forms that are monochromatic and brightly coloured. Among his own influences were the mounds of pigment found in bazaars in India. In his early works he imbued natural materials such as sandstone with raw powdered pigment of vivid hues, particularly red, yellow and blue, creating a feeling of inner radiance.

CINEMATOGRAPHY

Also having a powerful impact on my work were the films of Japanese filmmaker Akira Kurosawa (1910–98), particularly *Dreams* in which eight concurrent vignettes express a personal journey for the director. One of these, "The Peach Orchard," seems to come alive with the orchard in blossom, and I have wanted to evoke this in many colour projects. Even the gruesome US television show *CSI Miami*, which is shot with the most alluring coloured light (frequently solar or citrus yellows), has become a memorable influence banked for the future.

If you aim to observe the way colours behave whenever you go to films or an art gallery, you will gradually become more sophisticated in your understanding of them. The more knowledge you have about colour and its influence on your living environment, the better placed you will be to choose colours that will be right for you and your home.

HISTORICAL ARCHITECTURE AND DESIGN

This is another rich field of inspiration, which has greatly contributed to my colour ranges and ongoing projects. Designers are eternally looking into the past for visual design references for both fashion and interiors. From the frescoes of Pompeii and the decorative tiles of Persia to the cooler palettes of Wedgwood and Worcester ware, the past offers a wealth of colour inspiration.

Left: Visitors standing beside Yves Klein's "IKB" monochrome exhibit at the Guggenheim Museum in Bilbao.

POMPEII AND HERCULANEUM

With thick layers of ash having covered the towns of Herculaneum and Pompeii for nearly 1,700 years, it is a miracle that so much was preserved of the lives of the ancients. The towns' accidental rediscovery in the mid-eighteenth century allowed an astounding insight into the art, architecture and interior decoration of the Roman Empire. How incredible that nearly nine metres (thirty feet) of fine ash kept the colour of many of the walls in Pompeii the same as when they were painted, nearly two thousand years ago. The eyebrow-raising frescoes on the walls of the Stabian Baths have a fantastic palette of deep red, yellow ochre, luscious green and chocolate brown. They remain valuable suggestions for a multitude of decorative schemes today, as they are not only diverse, but intensely beautiful.

THE ORIENT

The Orient has been a great source of inspiration to me, as, indeed, it has been to British and European decorative artists through the centuries. From fourteenth-century Italian copies of Chinese silks, through the chinoiserie designs found in eighteenth-century rococo, to Persian pottery and tileworks that influenced the nineteenth-century English Arts and Crafts movement, the influence of the Orient has been immeasurable.

Chinese blue and white porcelain is for ever associated with the Ming dynasty (1368–1644), though it was still produced during the Qing dynasty (1644–1912). Qing dynasty porcelain from the Kangxi period (1662–1722) was noted for its pure white ground decorated with a brilliant sapphire blue, sometimes known as Nanking or Nankin blue.

Other wonderful colours were also associated with particular periods and designs through the centuries, as in China's monochrome wares. The soft grey-green colour known as celadon originated in a semi-translucent stoneware glaze from the Song dynasty (960–1279); imitations of this glaze were also produced later. Early in the Ming dynasty, glazes included celadon, cobalt blue, copper red, Imperial yellow (a colour China associated with its emperor) and turquoise. During the later Ming dynasty, apple green, deep purple, iron brown and iron red were added. More beautiful glazes appeared during the Qing dynasty, including robin's egg (speckled turquoise), peachbloom (mottled mushroom pink) and clair-de-lune (pale blue).

The Ming and Qing dynasties were also celebrated for their polychrome wares. During the Kangxi period, *famille vert* enamelled porcelain appeared, in translucent colours including apple green, iron-red, yellow, deep purple and violet-blue. Shortly after, *famille rose* porcelain was introduced, using opaque enamels including a dominant rose pink.

The Persians, unlike the Arabs and the Moors, were free to introduce animal life in their decoration of houses, and this mixture of subjects drawn from real life led to an unconventional style of ornament and a use of wonderful colours. Light green and turquoise was a favourite colour for Persian pottery. It was softer and paler that the Chinese variety, used in some brilliant Ming specimens.

Another legendary tint was aubergine (eggplant); it varied from a pink shade light in colour to a purplish bruise and a brownish violet.

GEORGIAN ENGLAND

As the social custom of taking afternoon tea increased in popularity during the eighteenth century, it made way for both Worcester and Wedgwood to produce more elaborate and decorative tea sets. Both potteries used a strong cobalt blue derivative as their signature colour, but through design development more eclectic palettes appeared.

At roughly the same time as British potteries were gaining international recognition, the successful family business of Robert and James Adam was reinforcing the popularity of neoclassicism in England and Scotland. Robert Adam (1728-92) sought inspiration from Italy and established the company's fame through his desire to design everything down to the smallest detail, ensuring a sense of unity in their designs.

The universal use of varying tones of green has inspired some of the colours in both my Architectural and Original ranges.

MODERNISM

Most of my sources of inspiration have had a heavy bias on colour in ornamental decoration. However, two notable architects working in the Modern movement of the twentieth century have become an undeniable source of reference through their ideas for new designs and colours.

One of the most important figures to demonstrate Modernist principles in his rejection of ornament and his belief that form follows function was the Swiss-born architect Le Corbusier (1887-1965). Le Corbusier was a pioneer in theoretical studies of modern design, extending his talents to urban planning, furniture design and painting. Although the majority of his architectural work was devoid of elaborate colour and was more based on the materials he used, he did experiment extensively with colour.

The Colour Keyboards collections he undertook with the Swiss wallpaper manufacturer Salubra appeal to me the most. He developed these novel prefabricated rolls of oil paint in order to avoid painting three coats of paint; however, the rolls were all monochrome. Le Corbusier then invented a sophisticated colour selection machine for the company's customers. Conceived as an instrument or a kind of book, which could be folded and unfolded up to four times, the invention provided the user with the possibility of comparing larger colour strips with smaller colour samples as well as with large colour sheets. Le Corbusier specified the colours of the different keyboards.

The colours that Corbusier was developing were directly influenced by the work of the Mexican architect Luis Barragán (1902-87), who in turn travelled to Europe to listen to lectures

Opposite: Detail of Persian tiles; an inspiring combination of aubergine (eggplant), light green and turquoise colours.

given by Le Corbusier. Barragán, whose buildings are renowned for their mastery of space and light, succeeded in creating his own version of modernism. He imbued the Modernist principles and International Style with the warmth and vibrancy of his native Mexico's popular culture. Transforming the Modernist ethos of a radical simplification of form, a rejection of ornament, and the use of glass, steel and concrete as preferred materials, Barragán added vivid colours and textural contrasts accentuating his buildings' natural surroundings. Most Modernist architects did not use much colour and this is why I admire Barragán so much. In a house in Mexico City, two tall pink walls created such a volume of colour that it reflected into the interior. His signature colours included Mexican pink, yellow and lilac, forming a distinctive and totally original style. Barragán describes his approach in the following way:"In alarming proportions the following words have disappeared from architectural publications: beauty, inspiration, magic, sorcery, enchantment, and also serenity, mystery, silence, privacy, astonishment. All of these have found a loving home in my soul."

By combining the austere architectural practices of Modernism with an abundance of colour, Barragán became skilled at manipulating light. The interiors of his buildings seem to have a softness and cosiness not associated with Modernist architecture. Primary colours in general are difficult to apply to a scheme, yet Luis Barragán always fills me with an enthusiastic belief that one day I will create an environment using a similar palette.

All styles and periods of art, design and architecture offer colour inspiration, and I have mentioned only a few of my favourites. They are an indication that one can be inspired by so many different eras even if they are not necessarily a style you like.

Above top: I like the beautiful balance of monochromatic colours used here by Jose Yturbe on a project in Mexico.
Above: Overscaled yellow door way in a neutral hallway leads to a colourful living space away from the heat.
Opposite: The simple colour composition on strong architectural elements underpins the genius of this Luis Barragán's geometric style.

NATURE

According to the French Impressionist painter Edouard Manet, "There are no lines in nature, only areas of colour, one against another." Colour surrounds us all the time, influencing the way we think, feel and act. Hence the more immediate inspiration for your scheme is nature. From complementary colours in flowers to the tones of leaves, trees and grass; and from the muted neutrals of sand and driftwood or the varying colours of rocks and minerals to the intense patterns and colours of animal skin and feathers, let nature work for you.

Nature's colors are familiar and have a widely accepted harmony but they also yield wonderful possibilities. One way to determine the colours you like from the vast amount of influences around you is to look at the details in nature – for example, the pattern of a pheasant feather or the inside of a seashell.

As with the influences already mentioned, it seems appropriate to share the key inspirations I have researched, primarily to explore tones for my paint ranges. As I grew up in Australia, it would have been difficult for me not to have sought inspiration from its incredible geographic features. Hot Earth, the muted, sludgy terracotta from my Original Colours, is based on the unique, striking and vivid colour of the Simpson Desert. The paints Eucalyptus, Reef, Deep Water Green and Shoredust all have connections with my life growing up on a cattle farm in northern New South Wales.

In complete contrast, the sacred Inner Hebrides island of Iona in Scotland is the source of one of only three true marbles in Britain – Iona marble. Found in a small geological outcrop at the south of the island, the beautiful green and white stone has a unique hue that is perfect to create a calm environment. The stone itself is supposedly endowed with supernatural powers, possibly making it the perfect colour choice for a psychic salon.

My Original Colours range is based heavily on colours inspired by nature. Pelican Throat, Euphorbia, Samphire, Impala, Squid Ink and Nebulus are just a few examples of the diversity the earth and its inhabitants can offer. I believe that if colours work naturally together in their environment – minerals with rocks, animal skins with feathers – they will work together well in an interior.

Opposite and above: Colours that occur together naturally in flora and fauna are easily understood and are often successful when transposed to other interior painted surfaces or schemes. A zebra stripe (above) could be easily the inspiration for a black and white spiral staircase sight line (opposite).

EVERYDAY CONSUMER PRODUCTS

These are generally overlooked because of their prosaic function and because they have become a customary part of our lives. Although familiar and commonplace, packaging design is an innovative and premier design industry. Objects can become mundane and inconspicuous, but I feel they offer intriguing and bold direction for colour inspiration. I am not alone in believing that – the trend for reinterpreting everyday products is increasing in popularity.

One of the best-selling items at The Conran Shop in both Europe and the United States is a gold porcelain vase, taken from the mould of a fabric-softener bottle. This vessel not only is novel but highlights the influence of consumer product design. An up-and-coming design company, Yoyo Ceramics, has reworked the familiar plastic Tupperware-style container in ceramic. This witty and colourful range is another example of the power that consumer objects have in our lives.

My wallpaper Liberation, which is now a design classic and a best-seller at Paint & Paper Library, was developed from a series of drawings I completed in 1992 with the Australian artist Ruark Lewis (exhibited at Galleria Mar Estrada, Spain) based on the layout of a French newspaper. By ignoring the way in which one reads, we created a design that unveiled the geometric shapes found in the division of the text, advertising and photographs to reveal a strangely familiar pattern from an ordinary everyday object.

Packaging graphic design is a highly competitive business with more emphasis on the brand itself – for example, the perfume industry. Each season, new brands and scents are launched and the packaging is eagerly anticipated.

When looking at the products around us, it is the patina, sheen, texture and saturation of colour that appeal to me. The allure and glossiness of products like the award-winning Apple iPod by Jonathan Ive, or the stealth and exclusivity of the latest scent or make-up packaging, are as seductive and addictive as they are desirable. The Japanese colourist Haruko Masuda has reflected traditional Japanese colours inspired from nature itself when designing NEC's N701i mobile phones. They provide an unusual and interesting juxtaposition of old and new, traditional and modern.

Orange is one of the most remarkable and powerful brands in the wireless telecommunication industry and in turn has recognized orange as an influential and luxurious colour. This is seen also in the packaging at Hermès, where the hue has been combined with the deepest brown. Equally recognizable is the black and white of Chanel. The impact of corporate colours on chainstores has a multitude of effects, drawing in customers and leading to an upturn in the use of ubiquitous colours in advertising, graphics, fashion, interiors and technology. But however ubiquitous or synonymous with a brand name they are, these colours can provide a sophisticated and fresh source of inspiration for your home colour scheme, the origin of which would never be recognized.

Opposite: The division of text advertising and photographs found in a French newspaper was the starting point for my geometric wallpaper design "Liberation". It is memorable and strangely familiar because the shapes are frequently seen when we read but not always noticed.

Above: I've always been inspired by how signs form fascinating patterns particularily when viewed in an unfamiliar language.

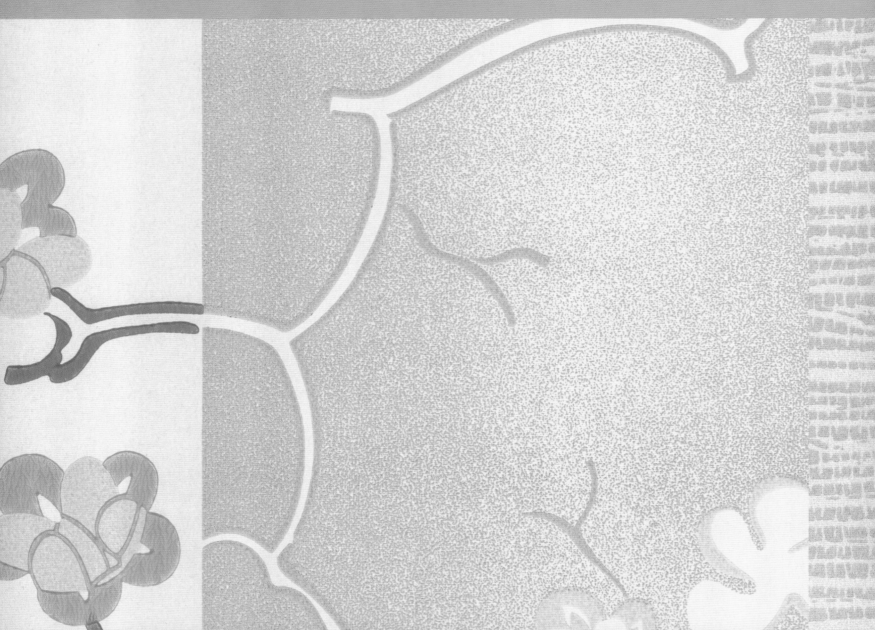

PRACTICAL INTERPRETATION

"Red is a colour I've felt very strongly about. Maybe red is a very Indian colour, maybe it's one of those things that I grew up with and recognize at some other level." **ANISH KAPOOR**

Once you have considered the various factors that will affect your scheme, have sought inspiration in a variety of places and have collected whatever you are using as a basis for the scheme, you are ready to create a mood board, the indispensable tool for any project. Gather together all the magazine tear sheets, book covers, photographs, postcards, driftwood, pebbles or other material you have collected for each particular room. Invariably the colour you covet most will jump out at you, providing not only a departure point for the scheme but also the accent colour itself.

PAINT SAMPLES

These colours will only become real once they have been translated into paint colours, which will be the basic elements of your mood board. I advise acquiring painted (rather than matched) colour charts, trials or references. It is usually best to cut up these charts, for example if you are using paints from my Architectural or Original ranges, and place the individual colours alongside your collected material, as the first step towards translating your choices into paint.

Experiment with the paint chips, moving them around and imagining how you would employ the colours in the room. Be free in your arrangement, allowing your personality to show through; improvise and analyse. Eventually you will be able to reduce your initial choice to about four – the accent colour which has already made itself evident and the various core colours. Although you haven't bought the paint yet, you do now have your first visual tool reflecting the desired result. This will be the basis of your mood board.

ELEMENTS OF A MOOD BOARD

Designers' mood boards are often elaborate, but even very simple ones are useful. A mood board essentially consists of samples of colours, patterns and textures that will be used in the room. Ideally, the size of the samples should be roughly in proportion to their use in the room, so floor coverings and ceiling and wall colours will be large, while accessories and trimmings will be small, with window treatments and upholstery somewhere in between. You could also arrange them to correspond to their positions in the room, with floor coverings at the bottom and ceiling colour at the top.

Use samples of the actual paint, fabric or carpet if you can, but where this is not feasible use colour samples that are as close as possible. The more representative you can make the mood board, the more likely you are to spot unsuccessful choices. And remember that the mood board does not mean the scheme is set in stone – feel free to make changes whenever and wherever you wish.

MAKING CHOICES

As your favourite colour palettes begin to emerge, how do you determine which colours will be the most successful? Frequently clients come to me in a state of what I call paint-analysis paralysis, even though they could have avoided the situation with a little expert guidance. Of course, the way we use colour in our homes will always be instinctive, as it is one of the greatest forms of individual expression – but the principles and techniques underlying how colours are applied and combined can be taught. The purpose of this chapter is to isolate and conquer some of the most common stumbling blocks, which stand between you and a wonderful colour scheme.

The old saying that home is where the heart is reflects how we usually choose colour – our choices clearly express

Opposite: A mood board can incorporate all the key elements of a room not just the flat surfaces. Use pictures of everyday objects housed in a favourite room such as china, table and glassware and build a colour scheme around it.

how we want to live. Home is where we are the most comfortable, and we have strong feelings about this personal space. A house or apartment provides a sanctuary from frenetic everyday life as well as a secure base from which we can go out into the world and fulfil our ambitions and desires. It is therefore important to find the palettes that will support these functions of the home, easing tensions and creating a feeling of harmony and security.

Colour not only reflects personal tastes but actually influences mood and behaviour. This has been recognized for centuries but it is still an area where little is understood. Colour analysis is a complex topic, and many people have misconceptions about our emotional, physical and behavioural responses to different hues. Although colour is physically processed by the eyes, it is not purely a visual phenomenon; intricate psychological processes also have a bearing on our perception of it.

Colour defines the world we live in. Our eyes register the colour of an object before we see through to the object itself and notice its form. We are not initially attracted to lines or shapes (though a designer will generally try to synchronize colour and form), so it is inevitable that the predominant colours of a room will have a visual impact before the furnishings themselves.

As well as having an overall aesthetic value, colour enhances the details and materials used to accessorize a room. With careful planning, it can also be manipulated to improve the proportions of a room and the relationship between space and personal possessions. Choosing the right colour scheme imposes order on the elements of a room, or a home, marking boundaries and defining spaces and functions. To devise a scheme that will work well in your home, I believe that the most crucial aspects of design that you should consider are light, environment, rhythm and balance, proportion and scale, and emphasis and harmony, all of which are covered on the following pages.

Opposite: Dark woodwork doesn't necessarily mean gloomy. Use laquered and glossy doors or gilded moulding to enhance and bounce natural light around a room to great effect.

LIGHT

Without light there is no colour. We see the colour of an object only when it is bathed in natural light. The English physicist Sir Isaac Newton observed that a ray of "white light" (daylight) passing through a prism is broken into the spectral hues. White light is, therefore, a mixture of all the colours of the rainbow, each of which has a different wavelength. As light strikes a surface, the surface absorbs only the wavelengths that match its own atomic structure, reflecting the rest.

When this reflected light enters the eye, receptors in the retina begin to decode the information and then send messages to the brain, which identifies the wavelength as being a particular colour. The most visually demanding wavelength is the longest one – red – because the eye has to make the most adjustment in order to pass on the message to the brain. Red is therefore perceived as a more stressful colour than, say, green, which requires almost no adjustment by the eye.

CHANGING DAYLIGHT

Light is obviously an important consideration when choosing colour. Natural daylight is regarded as the best form of illumination for interiors because it reveals true colours. Although the intensity of daylight varies according to where you live and the orientation of your windows, it is necessary to balance warmth and coolness in both daylight and artificial lighting. Different lighting conditions affect colours in a variety of ways. For example, in dim light red, orange and yellow appear darker whereas blue and green appear lighter. Black takes on a grey tone in bright white light or daylight.

On page 22, I explained the need to monitor how and when natural daylight affects a room, so by now you will hopefully have studied the light conditions within each room in the morning, at noon, at sunset and in the evening. Because the angle of the light changes through the day, certain wavelengths predominate at particular times. Cool blues are a feature of morning light, while at noon the light is neutral (white), before gradually getting warmer through the afternoon so that intense reds and yellows predominate just before sunset, to be followed by the cool light of twilight. On a cloudy day, the light is cooler than on a clear day.

Daylight also changes through the year, as the earth proceeds through its solar orbit and its tilted axis points towards or away from the sun. Be aware of all these challenges of the light – although you can't change your colour scheme according to the time of day, weather or season, you can take account of what conditions predominate over a period of time, and at what time of day you will most use the room.

ARTIFICIAL LIGHTING

As well as natural light, think about the type of artificial lighting you will be using. Not only the type of fitting – such as table or floor lamps, wall sconces, spotlights, uplighters, accent lights – but also the type of light source you use will greatly influence the atmosphere.

Candlelight is the warmest light source, while conventional tungsten bulbs are nearly as warm, being predominantly in the yellow to red part of the spectrum. Both candles and tungsten bulbs cast a gentle, warm light, making upholstered surfaces appear softer. This will enhance warm colours like reds, oranges and yellows but will make the cooler shades such as blues and greens less appealing. Like tungsten, halogen bulbs are a type of incandescent lighting, but halogen casts a cooler, whiter light that is closer to daylight and is crisp and sparkling, making colours seem clearer.

Fluorescent light casts a bluer light and can alter the hues in a room. This type of lighting is mainly used in commercial settings and in areas of the home where strong, utilitarian overall lighting is required. Although there are many different types of fluorescent light, the one most commonly used lacks the warm colours of the spectrum. It tends to enhance only blues and greens, while rendering reds, oranges and yellows dull. If you are using fluorescent lights in the home, choose "full-spectrum" or daylight varieties, which enhance all colours.

In my opinion, a combination of more than one type of light source – for example, halogen spotlights combined with tungsten bulbs in individual table or floor lamps – works best. A failsafe option is to have all lighting computer-controlled or on individual dimmer switches that will modulate and manage the lighting to create an ambience, change the mood, tailor lighting conditions to the time of day and enhance the natural properties of your dominant core colour.

> To create a pleasurable glow or bring an air of romance to a colour scheme, try the professional trick of surrounding your core colours with darker or complementary hues, creating an attractive luminosity.

> One method I use to predict the effects of light in a room is to paint the inside of a box (an old shoebox without the lid is ideal) in the desired colour(s). Viewed from above, it will mimic in miniature the effect of an overhead light source. Observe how the colour reflects light onto itself and intensifies in appearance accordingly. You can even cut holes in the sides of the box to represent windows. Look at the ways in which the shadow falls and see how the depth of colour changes fom side to side – how it hangs like smoke in the corners and how it mimics the deeper and softer recesses of a room when viewed from different angles. Use this effective method when planning your lighting to help you anticipate where you will need to either increase or decrease the intensity of light to achieve the desired effect.

Opposite: Mirrored or sheeted glass walls can also assist in concealing artificial light sources creating an atmospheric feeling of efficiency, clarity and space.

ENVIRONMENT

Because light has such a profound effect on the way colour is perceived, the location of your home is another important factor in your choice of colour scheme, since this determines the quality of natural light it receives. If you live in a temperate climate, the light will never be as bright as it is nearer the equator – and vice versa. Remember that if you are tempted to try to re-create at home the sensations of the flora and fauna, food, wine and buildings you fall in love with on your travels. Finding the actual colours is not difficult these days, because so many diverse ranges are now available, offering anything from Roman reds or Turkish blues to Indian pinks or Chinese yellows. But although the colours used in, say, Mexico or Marrakesh are fantastic in isolation or in the right context, their beautiful rawness can just look lurid in the more delicate light of northern Europe or the more northerly United States. Similarly, a delicate and subtle Scandinavian colour palette could look insipid in the strong light of southern California or Spain. Don't let this stop you from seeking inspiration for colour schemes on your travels – just be aware of the difficulties in translation.

To establish the most comfortable, appropriate and aesthetic environment, the best approach is to be guided by your home's architecture (both interior and exterior) and also its setting. The most flattering and subtle colour schemes take into account the surrounding landscape, rural or urban, as well as the architecture and period of neighbouring homes. For a historic home a colour scheme that evokes the period and style will be rich with precedent and can look comfortably instinctual. In elegant London streets, for example, the browning leaves of the great plane trees, towering tan and gold, subtly set off the rows of elegant Regency houses with their understated front doors, veiled windows and cream stucco façades, all smooth and sleek with the eggshell sheen of property. Victorian architecture, on the other hand, can sustain bolder colours and patterns than eighteenth- or early nineteenth-century buildings.

Earth tones, in my opinion, are always a good choice in natural, wooded areas, as they look appropriately organic. One of my favourite buildings is Falling Water, in western Pennsylvania, designed in 1935 for the Kaufmann family by the American architect Frank Lloyd Wright. Responding to the clients' love of a waterfall on a stream called Bear Run, Wright cantilevered the house over the falls so that it seems to belong intrinsically to its setting. One of Wright's most acclaimed works, it is a superb example of organic architecture, which promotes harmony between man and nature. Falling Water's original furnishings, still there today, were designed by Wright to fit unobtrusively into the surroundings, while the colours he chose were warm and bright, to offset the deep greys of the local sandstone and the reinforced concrete used for the house.

I always feel it is better to blend colours in easy harmonies than to contrast them like a visual architectural puzzle. (However, strong contrasts are not without their uses. I remember a village in the west of Ireland where the houses were painted in an array of brightly contrasting colours that could best be described as curiously inept. As the story goes, the reason for such vibrant exterior paint choices was that when staggering home after a late-night drinking session, one can recognize one's own home more easily!)

RHYTHM AND BALANCE

These are extremely important in creating a feeling of unity within an interior. Being methodical in your approach to colour brings authority to a scheme. Because the human eye is initially drawn to colour and not individual objects, using a rhythmical but balanced approach creates visual order, marking boundaries and defining areas.

Start with rhythm, which is introduced through the repetition of colours within a room. This extremely useful technique brings unity to a scheme while at the same time

Opposite, clockwise from bottom left: Frank Lloyd Wright's own house, Falling Water, and an interior and exterior view of Storer House that he designed for John Storer – both quintessential examples of architecture intrinsic to their surroundings and settings.

conveying a feeling of tempo and movement. The aim is to create a progression of tones, using tints and shades of your pure core colour and possibly also some neutrals. My Architectural Colours range of paints has been devised to make this simple, as it comprises not only tones progressing from light (for the ceiling) to dark (for the floor) but also the same hue in different intensities.

Using a tonal progression of your colour is preferable to placing contrasting colours - yellow, red, violet, blue and green, for instance - side by side as the eye-brain function takes a little longer to translate the impression of contrasting colours than it does for tones of one hue.

When you are using this technique of sequencing tints, shades and neutrals throughout the room, it is generally best to use only a few hues, as this creates better visual unity. As mentioned earlier, if you do wish to take a more adventurous approach to the use of colour, I advise you to study the works of artists and designers who have experimented with revealing the power of colour and its combinations.

At this stage, the tonal base you have prepared has rhythm but it is flat, and so the next step is to create the illusion of space and depth. You do this by creating balance in the scheme through the use of up to two accent colours. As well as adding equilibrium and poise, this helps to define the scheme as a whole. It is at this moment that the ambience you are trying to achieve using colour will finally appear and true personal expression will be revealed.

You can add the accent colours (colours used in small quantities to lift or to add punch to a colour scheme) either symmetrically or asymmetrically. For symmetrical balance, arrange the accent colours as mirror images of each other. For asymmetrical balance, place the accent colours randomly around the room, preferably in the furnishings or architectural details.

I don't recommend using more than two different accent colours, as this could create too confused a visual effect. The most successful projects I have achieved have been the ones I kept simple, applying rhythm through core tonal values and then adding a limited number of accent colours for balance.

Above: Coral accent colours derived from the papered walls form the core colour scheme for the soft furnishing and bed covers in this spare room.
Opposite: Grand classical murals are the perfect setting for luxurious fabrics and richly decorated textures in this bedroom's soft furnishing, rug and carpet scheme.

PROPORTION AND SCALE

The proportions of a room and the scale of its furnishings are aspects that are vital to consider when planning a decorating scheme. The colours you need to choose, and the way you use them, will vary according to these factors. However, trying to imagine how a colour will look when used on one or more surfaces is very difficult.

In fact, the trickiest part of choosing colour is making the conceptual leap from a tiny two-dimensional chip of paint to the vast amount seen on a whole wall. Buying numerous sample pots helps to avoid major mistakes, yet they will not reveal how this colour will look on a grand scale. No colour works in isolation, and so daubing the wall with testers, although it will help, will not necessarily give you the desired effect because so many factors will come into play when you actually decorate. Therefore, keep in mind the following advice:

> When you are using two or more colours, an illusion of depth can occur, sometimes even creating a distorted perspective. For example, if yellow is placed near a blue-violet colour, the yellow becomes very "active" and stands out.

> When colours, particularly white, are used in the same proportions, the effect is too static. Think about the actual area of the wall that will be painted in the desired colour, and its scale in relation to the room's other elements, such as the architectural detailing or the size of the windows. Will your colour choice affect these aspects? What proportion of the room's flat surfaces will it take up?

> The larger the room, the brighter that intense colours will appear, while at the same time being less demanding than in smaller rooms. Therefore, larger rooms will benefit from a deeper shade.

> The scale of the furniture and furnishings is also very important. A colour can appear to operate cohesively on one surface but may alter dramatically when placed side by side with your favourite armchair or carpet. An oversized sofa, individual armchairs or an overbearing dining table can have a visual effect on the colour of the walls. They can also help if you are using the interior designer's trick of "overscaling," to make a small room seem larger. (And in a big room, such large pieces are, of course, essential if they are not to look silly.)

Above: Earthware pots, jugs and dishes create the perfect balance of tone and texture for this solar yellow back kitchen area.

Opposite: A graphic colour counterpoint of citrus yellow and rust is balanced beautifully in the scale and proportion of sofas, walls and cushions.

> Take into account the colours and patterns of the accessories as these too have a visual impact and can detract from or enhance the walls.

> Large sofas with small cushions create a strong focal point; huge rugs on bare floors or patterned carpets are other important, large-scale elements.

> Use the tone and placement of the paint to adjust the apparent proportions of a room. Painting the floor and/or skirting (baseboard) in a tone darker than those of the ceiling and mouldings can make the room appear larger or taller, even if the difference is only slight. Remember to include the architrave woodwork around the doors and windows.

> I prefer for an undersized room to be decorated in a lighter hue or a large-scale pattern, which can then be emphasized with a darker colour.

EMPHASIS AND HARMONY

Creating emphasis is a similar process to using the accent colour to give balance to a scheme, but it also concerns the textures, sheens and finishes of the walls and how they work with the floors and with the adjacent walls of other rooms. The aim is to create areas of importance upon which to focus.

ADDING EMPHASIS

There are a number of ways to create emphasis, so try some of the following techniques:

> Because colour has the wonderful quality of attracting attention before outlines or shapes are registered, it can be particularly effective to combine large areas of one colour with small areas of another, or to combine soft colours with hard ones. Using contrasting colours can be very striking (see page 130), although I don't normally use this method myself.

> Introducing pattern to a scheme through the use of wallpaper creates another level of focus. Wallpaper has seen a renaissance over the past few years, and more and more people are using pattern in a contemporary way, spreading energy throughout a room or adjoining passageways and communal spaces. I like to alternate patterned walls in rooms with plainer ones.

> Texture has long been used to create emphasis. The rougher or more uneven the texture, the greater the impact on the eye. However, rough textures make colour look darker – the more the texture is fractured, the darker the hue will appear. Remember this if your wall surfaces are uneven.

> Introduce different sheen levels and textures, such as fabric-covered, veneered or lacquered walls, from room to room. I find a series of rooms are infinitely more charming if there is some variety in wall finishes. There are various instruments available to decorate with, so why not explore them? Deeper colours have a sexy self regard when they are lacquered and glossy. Equally metallic golds and silver can add a burnished beauty that is a million miles away from an otherwise ordinary room's austere plainness.

CREATING HARMONY

Just as a symphony is made more interesting through the repetition of the melody by different instruments, so you might employ the same colour scheme throughout your home but vary the wall finishes – say, from a dynamic wallpapered entry hall to fabric-covered walls in the dining room and a painted study. This creates an overall harmony that pulls the whole scheme together. A cohesive or uniform flooring will also do this, while gently assisting the transition between rooms.

In conclusion, remember to include the following elements when creating a new scheme:

> Repeat the core colour to create rhythm.

> Use accent colours to add depth and balance.

> Graduate the tones vertically from floor to ceiling to create the most natural look.

Above: The graphic painted horizontal stripes have perfectly accentuated the architectural rises of this modern staircase adding emphasis and style using contrast and pattern.

COLOUR ASSOCIATIONS

"I've handled colour as a man should behave. You may conclude that I consider ethics and aesthetics as one." **JOSEF ALBERS**

Colour has always fascinated me, and I am not alone, as it has always been regarded as one of life's mysteries. Nearly every civilization or culture has colours associated with it, though often only expressed in simple terms such as dark and light. Historically, artists adopted the principles put forward by Aristotle, that the basic colours were those of the earth's four main elements – fire, water, earth and air – and were mixtures of lightness and darkness. It was only when Newton made his discoveries (see page 55) two thousand years later in the seventeenth century that these colour theories were challenged. Since the twentieth century, interest in colour has risen to such dizzy heights that colour theory has re-emerged and is being used in a more positive way.

CHARACTERISTICS OF COLOURS

Colour influences every aspect of our lives, though often the significance of particular hues changes as they go in and out of fashion. One of the main functions of colour, I believe, is to provide information – visually and psychologically – through our behavioural, emotional and physical reactions to it. Colour is not the same for everyone, and reactions can be individual and instinctive. As well as the actual hue of an object, we respond immediately to the colour's tonal value and its saturation (purity, brightness or intensity). These visual qualities of the colour can take precedence over the period, design and placement of the object.

At Paint & Paper Library we have broken down colour to a more manageable size using the colour categories listed on the following pages. Because the research into colour psychology is extensive, I have applied general theories to the categories to help you come to the final hurdle of choosing colour.

Right: The colours around us create an emotional as well as physical response. A warm yellow blanket is heavenly to wrap up in on a cold winter's night

CITRUS YELLOW

In its pure primary form, citrus yellow is a bright, happy, sunny and stimulating hue that naturally creates a warm and optimistic environment. Historically, yellow has symbolized the beginning of spring, which has also meant hope and joy. The qualities of yellow are endless and varied. Through research, yellow has been shown to promote the assimilation of new ideas related to intellectual and expressive pursuits. Yellow is also thought to stimulate memory, judgement and decision-making. It represents a cheerful, hopeful and organized environment and, more bizarrely, is also said to aid the digestion.

The colours in this category – which include Chinese Emperor, Othman Brae and Hathaway – when used with plenty of light are particularly marvellous in entry halls, breakfast and morning rooms and studies. Use yellow in moderation, however. I do not recommend it for the bedroom, as it can prove too stimulating for the nervous system unless balanced and harmonized with another core colour such as silver or green.

Opposite: This clever yellow canopy, designed by Luis Barragán, transmits a marvellous rhythm of tones on an ascending staircase.

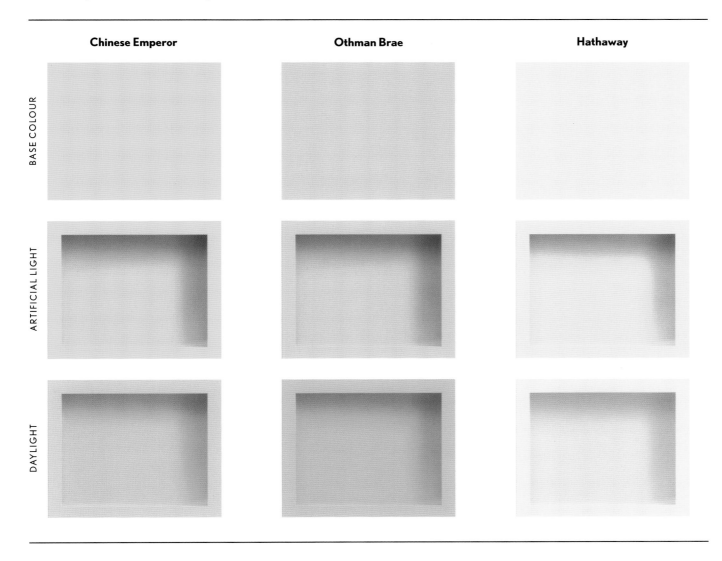

	Chinese Emperor	Othman Brae	Hathaway
BASE COLOUR			
ARTIFICIAL LIGHT			
DAYLIGHT			

This page: The yellow skylight and gold panel create a sunny aspect to an otherwise dim subterranean hallway.

OCHRE

Derived from the pigments of both ochre and raw sienna, the colours in this category create a perfect background for tweedy browns, travertine marble and honey-coloured matting and flooring. I am particularly fond of this group of colours, which range from mocha-latte, creamy colours through to earthier variants inspired by nature and dried bones. The natural pigment raw sienna is a form of limonite clay with a yellow-brown colour, which comes from the ferric oxides in it. It was one of the first to be used by humans and is found in many ancient cave paintings. The tones adapted from this pigment are much softer than the citrus yellows but have similar qualities.

Softer than yellow but far from bland, these earthy biscuit and cappuccino shades are sumptuous and mellow. They produce the same behavioural and emotional reactions as yellow, though perhaps not as intense, and I have used hues from this category in libraries, studies and stairwells. Originally found in servants' quarters of grand houses because they were cheaper to produce, these ubiquitous toasts look good virtually anywhere in the home and are particularly valuable for warming up rooms that don't get any sunshine. Shades such as Divine Brown, Dordogne and Paper are perennial favourites. When direct light hits these colours they take on a beautiful rawness.

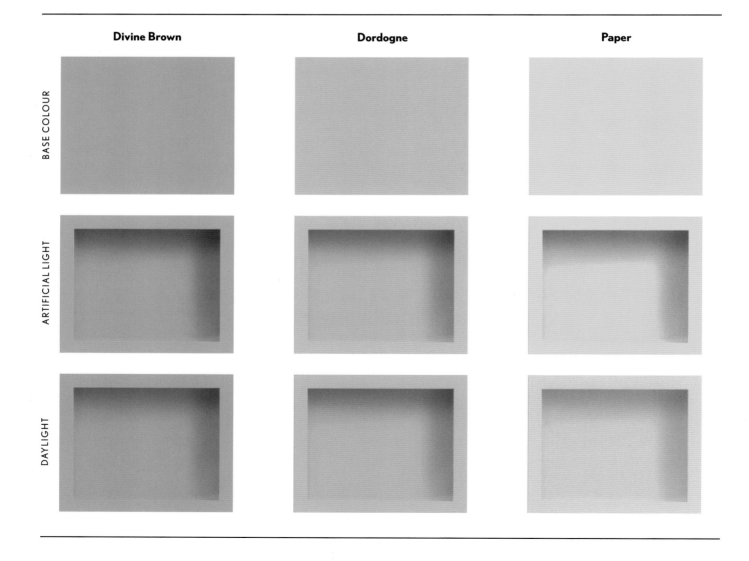

	Divine Brown	**Dordogne**	**Paper**
BASE COLOUR			
ARTIFICIAL LIGHT			
DAYLIGHT			

Above: The raw and natural pigments of the orche family are perfect for creating a balance that is both comfortably soft on the eye and mellow in temperature and tone.

Above: Ochre colours have found their way into pivotal positions in the house. Brown sugar, honey and mocha are all deeply delicious especially when enveloping a room used for relaxed entertaining.

Left: Earthy biscuit tones warm up a corridor that is deprived of natural light.

BUFF

This broad category ranges from sandy, sludgy tones to greys. Because it is so diverse, emotional reactions or specific qualities cannot be attributed to it. However, as the tones are derived from yellows, whites, blacks and greens, the list of benefits is endless. Light brown or tan has often symbolized genuineness, and the brown pigment from which it is derived, which represents comfort, endurance, stability and simplicity, is one of the favourite colours of men all over the world. Grey is associated with independence, self-reliance and self-control, and the category as a whole is perceived as dignified, official and intelligent but also high-tech.

When decorating I have used my favourite Truffle, Tarlatan and Estuary time and time again. These buff tones allow you to create a strong yet calm atmosphere in which warmer accent colours allow for a sophisticated and sometimes traditional appearance. Though often used in very contemporary interiors, this category of colours can be interpreted as transcending fashion.

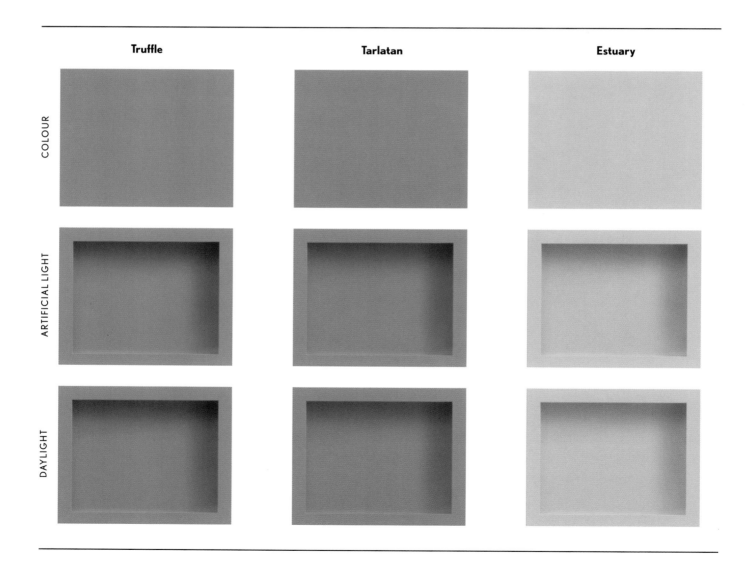

	Truffle	Tarlatan	Estuary
COLOUR			
ARTIFICIAL LIGHT			
DAYLIGHT			

Above: Gritty rendering can be so attractive especially on surface where the eye and hand have rested before. Variations of greige are one of the most popular neutral colour palettes.

SAGE AND OLIVE

Many people cite green as their favourite colour both in fashion and in home decoration. Green represents nature, the environment, health, good luck, renewal, youth, vigour, generosity and fertility. On top of all that, it is one of the most refreshing yet calming and comforting colours in the spectrum, promoting deep, slow breathing.

I have used many of the colours in this category to create an atmosphere of joy and lightness, but the darker hues have the opposite effect and are more sobering and sedative. Decorating with green creates a fresh, outdoorsy feeling and it is a great colour to decorate with if you work in a city because of its association with rural nature. What I call classic country-politan, these gumboot sage and olive greens, such as Horneblend, Both Barrels and Iona Marble, make a perfect choice for bedrooms, boot rooms (mudrooms), sitting rooms and libraries, as they are equally at home in town or country.

Opposite: Some of the most versatile colours in the spectrum, sage and olive greens epitomize the perfect country-politan – ideal whether in the town or country.

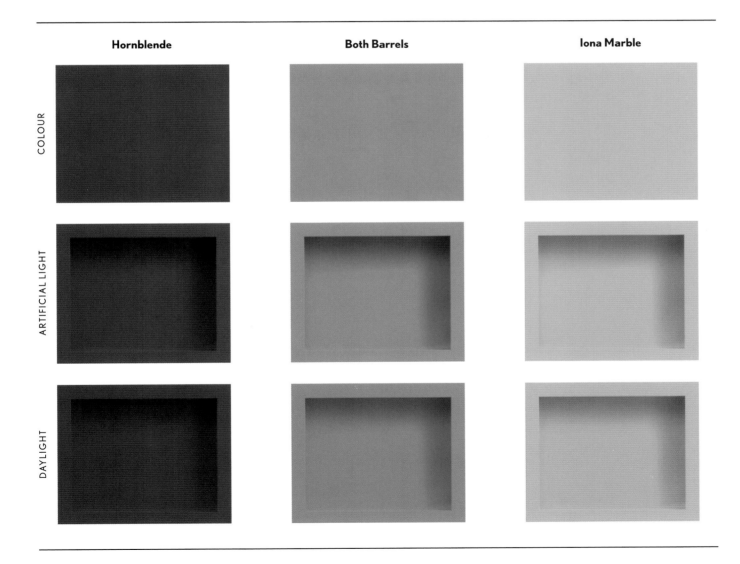

	Hornblende	Both Barrels	Iona Marble
COLOUR			
ARTIFICIAL LIGHT			
DAYLIGHT			

VERT

Possessing the same elements as a hearty green salad, the Vert category has all the associations and qualities of the greens discussed in the Sage and Olive category (see above), but more accentuated. Unapologetically clubby and suited to formal libraries or grand dining rooms, the richer heraldic greens in this category can be balanced by using a few paler tones in the room. Pure green has a neutral (medium) wavelength, which is easy on the human eye as we don't have to struggle to accept it – which perhaps explains why Hunter Dunn, Chelsea Green and Fennel, all in this category, are three of the most popular shades in the Original Colours range. The lighter shades in this category have proved perfect for children's bedrooms, more often boys' than girls'. On the whole, the colours in this category can be used as either accent or core colours and are thoroughly adaptable, whether used on planters in the conservatory or the kitchen dresser.

Opposite: Traditional and classic the formal vert greens have all the majestic qualities of a towering plane tree in full summer heat. Used here, in two shades of the same colour the mood remains fresh and not too sombre.

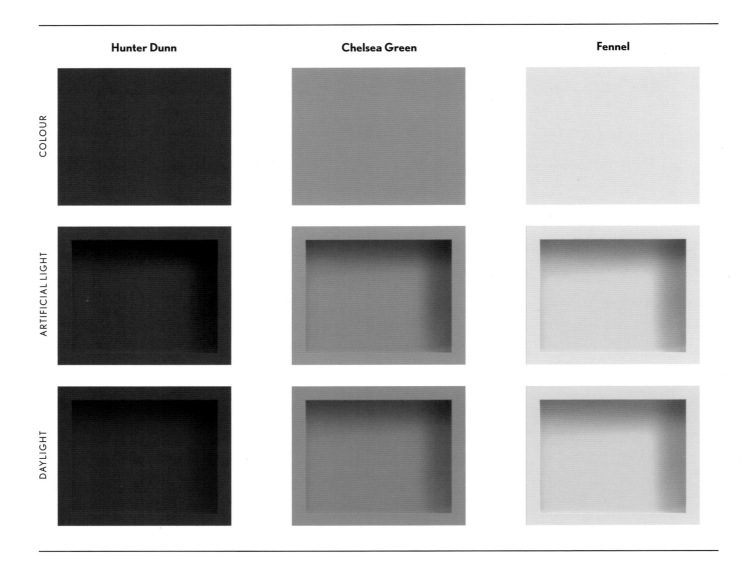

	Hunter Dunn	Chelsea Green	Fennel
COLOUR			
ARTIFICIAL LIGHT			
DAYLIGHT			

AQUA

Having grown up in Australia, I inevitably feel an affinity with wide azure skies and turquoise seas, that remind me of my homeland. Like greens, aqua evokes calm and serenity. The magic is endless not only because there are many different subtle shades of aqua, but also because it promotes both physical and mental relaxation, combining the therapeutic calming qualities of both the blues and the greens.

My favourites, Sobek, Storm and Quench the Gloom, have great tonal values and are a good place to start when experimenting with stronger colours.

Opposite: Aqua is the colour perhaps the most readily requested for bathrooms and utility rooms. Equally appropriate in a spare room or drawing room these hybrid blues/ greens are one of the easiest to incorporate into any contemporary colour scheme.

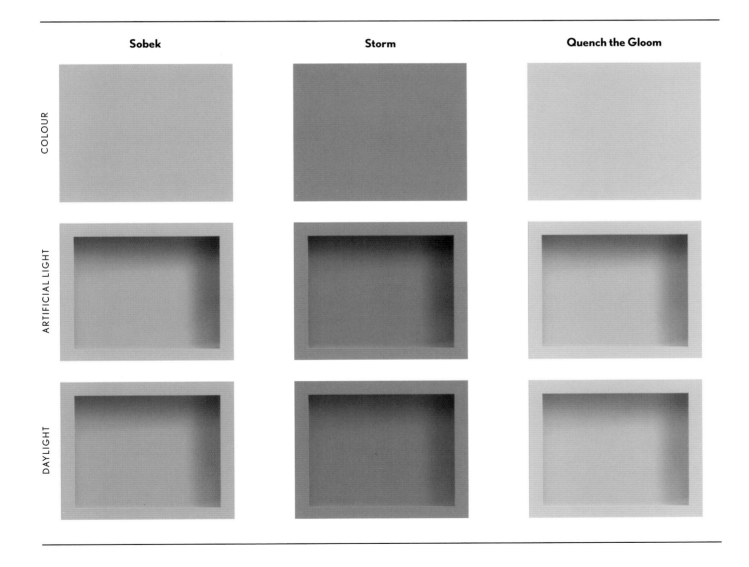

	Sobek	Storm	Quench the Gloom
COLOUR			
ARTIFICIAL LIGHT			
DAYLIGHT			

SEVRE

Throughout the centuries blue has been regarded as a spiritual colour, representing immortality in China, holiness in Judaism and Krishna in Hinduism. Vivid blue pigment, used in tempera paint, was one of the most precious of any artists' materials, often exceeding the price of gold. In the eighteenth century, fine French porcelain from Sèvres was renowned for its rich background colours, including the dark blue known as bleu lapis.

Blue is regal, exclusive and special, with the greatest degrees of intensity. If you get the right level of darkness in a particular shade of blue, it can encourage a deep and peaceful sleep. For the best effect, consider limiting the most intense shades to rooms that get a lot of sun. Blue Vein can look dramatic in a formal drawing room or a smart dining room against the family silver. I have even seen it deployed in a contemporary study, where it disguised the bleak edges of the day by confidently evoking summer skies. Tablecloth or Spur, on the other hand are perfect hues for a utility room or bathroom, casting a serene and calm light.

Opposite: Cooler than aqua this crisp china blue is used to great effect as a punctuation mark in a narrow passageway. A space where one can feel the spirit of the colour without having to linger.

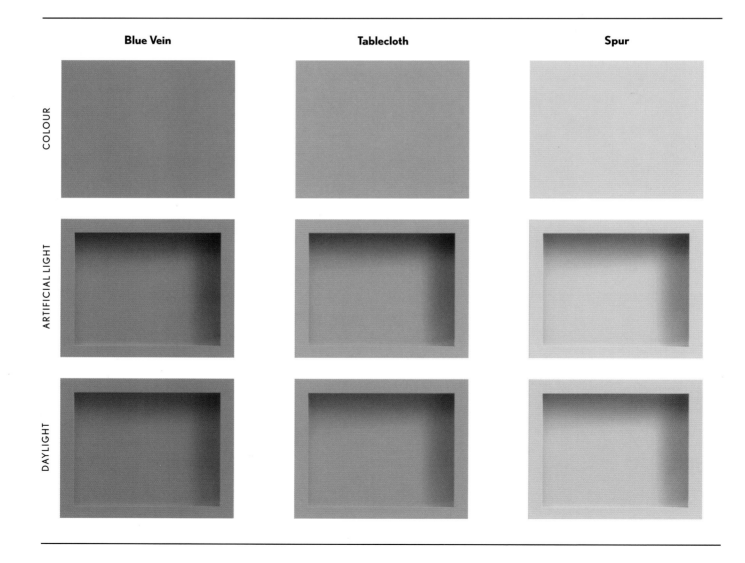

	Blue Vein	Tablecloth	Spur
COLOUR			
ARTIFICIAL LIGHT			
DAYLIGHT			

Above: Gunmetal blue is a great masculine colour for a room suffering from poor natural light. The boundaries of the room can spookily disappear into infinity especially at night. This bathroom would be wonderful lit only by candles at night.

Opposite: The delicate blue of this pretty wallpaper is the perfect foil for the worn surfaces where the eye and hand have rested before. The use of fragments and textures of colour illustrate a sensitive approach to the passing of time.

LAVENDER AND ROSA

Think puddles of pink coulis with purple aubergines (eggplants) – the colours are feminine and glamorous without being too frilly. They are not only fantastically versatile but wildly romantic and youthful. Steeped in history, violet has long been regarded as an exotic colour, representing royalty or clergy. Like ultramarine, the process in which the pigment was made was very expensive and so the colour was available only to the rich. Subliminally it now represents wealth, not just in monetary terms but also spiritually, relating to self-knowledge and spiritual awareness. Being one of the "cooler" colours, it creates a restful atmosphere, making it perfect for a bedroom.

Pink is a warmer colour but has similar effects to that of violet. It is also welcoming and soothing, having an affectionate and youthful aura while also being romantic and sexy. It is more suited to a subtle, thoughtful and serene environment and is perfect for a boudoir, dressing room, nursery or child's bedroom. Plum Brandy, Sugared Violet and Rouge, my favourites, are superb as accent colours inside bookshelves and cupboards.

Opposite: This hot pink welcoming passage is loaded with an alluring charm and creates exotic pleasure for the eye.

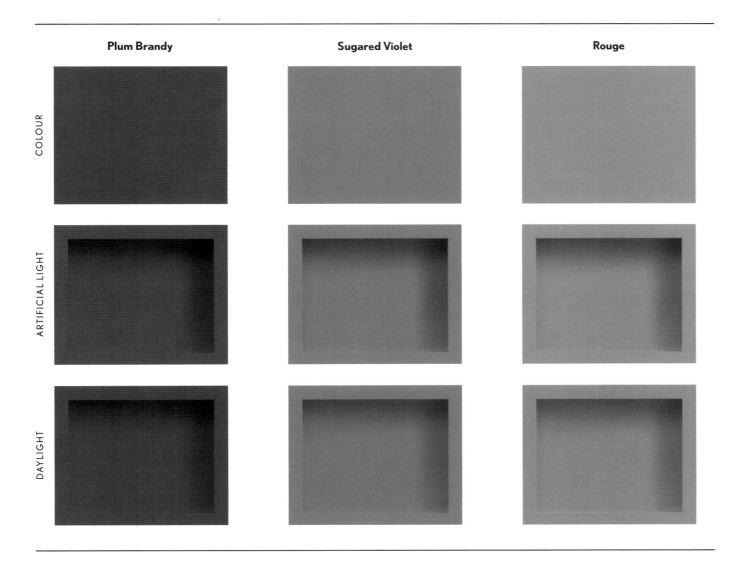

	Plum Brandy	Sugared Violet	Rouge
COLOUR			
ARTIFICIAL LIGHT			
DAYLIGHT			

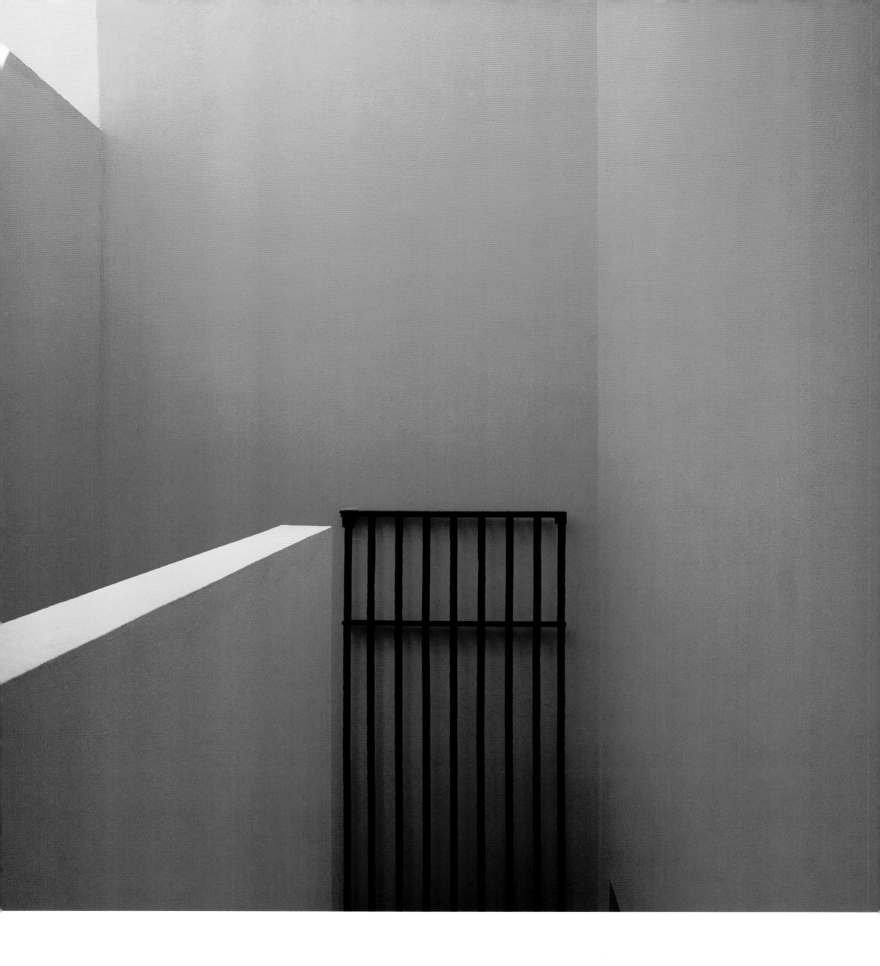

Opposite: Strong Mexican sunlight creates a chromatic crescendo of hot rhubarb pink tones that reinforce the strong geometric sight lines of a striking staircase.

Above: The decorative Pompeii painting and murals in this Roman bathroom are a great way to reduce the large expansive area for intimate and personal relaxation.

SCARLET AND RUST

My inspirations for this group of colours came from marmalade and burnt toast and also from the rock and sand formations of the Central Australian deserts. Because red is the most demanding on the eye, it immediately grabs your attention; it can even raise the blood pressure and heart rate. Throughout the centuries red has symbolized love, luck, passion, dynamism, courage and vitality. Combining the finer qualities of red and yellow, orange is competent, happy and forgiving as a hue, with the ability to fight depression and cultivate good humour.

Both red and orange are regarded as warming and energizing, but because they have a strong "personality" they must be used wisely or they can make spaces look small and oppressive. I prefer to use red and orange more as accent colours in dining rooms or kitchens, their value in promoting social activity and stimulating the appetite making them well suited to these rooms. The rust palette has proved to be fantastic in bedrooms, hallways, dining rooms and sitting rooms. Colours such Hot Earth, Very Well Read and Elizabethan Red are passion, especially when lacquered or glossy.

Opposite: Red is a tricky colour to coordinate on the woodwork. The Lamp Black gloss on the architrave and doors in this French kitchen beautifully acts as the supporting role of a shadow line.

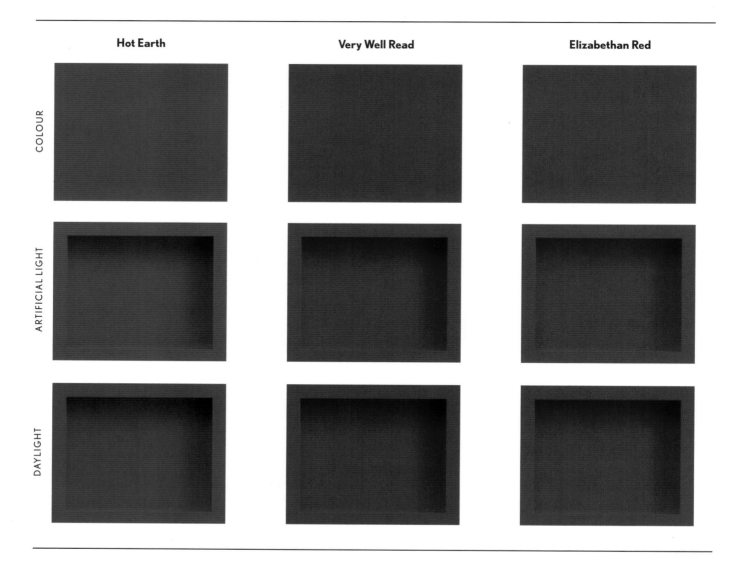

	Hot Earth	Very Well Read	Elizabethan Red
COLOUR			
ARTIFICIAL LIGHT			
DAYLIGHT			

Above: Complex and traditional, the dramatic rust stairwell lit more like a dim museum than a hallway, manages to evoke all the mystery of another generation.

Opposite: The cinematic qualities of this picture are largely due to the fabulous reddish brown colour of the rendered walls, as if painted with baked earth.

ZEBRA

According to the English writer G.K. Chesterton, "White... is not a mere absence of colour; it is a shining and affirmative thing, as fierce as red, as definite as black... God paints in many colours; but He never paints so gorgeously, I had almost said so gaudily, as when He paints in white." In the colour spectrum, white is the union of all colours. The reason it never goes out fashion is that it matches everything. Symbolizing purity, simplicity, innocence, hope and birth, it creates feelings of peace and comfort and dispels despair. It was the most widely used and best-loved colour of the Modernist movement and is employed today to create minimalist interiors. Because

it is unaffected by light, owing to its reflective abilities, it has associations with both summer and winter.

There are, in fact, a multitude of different shades of white. My Architectural Colours range offers a way of employing some of these, which is particularly effective when using paint to pick out ornate plasterwork or mouldings. Whites can be used in any room, but remember that although they can be peaceful, they can encourage feelings of isolation or create

Opposite: Black comes in all sorts of degrees and tones; the natural nuances of slate and stone can form the most beautiful blueish tints especially when wet.

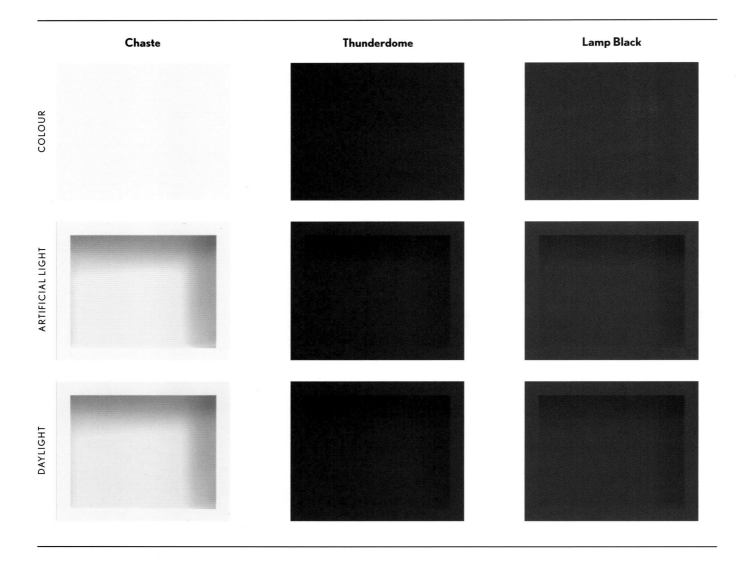

too clinical a look. The palest off-white in my Original Colours range is called Chaste. I have never been a fan of the harsh contrasts created by using a meretricious dazzling white – it has an awful brightness of purpose when used on woodwork throughout the home, as if it's pale with anger.

The antithesis of white, black absorbs all the colours of the spectrum and has the capacity to evoke strong emotions, initially by grabbing the attention. It can feel calming and protective, yet it does have strong associations with death and mourning in nearly all cultures. It is also glamorous, sophisticated, modern, creative and infinite.

A black mark on a page recedes into the background while a white line occupies the foreground, so don't be deceived into thinking that black will make the room feel smaller. In certain light these rooms can appear infinite. The boundaries become blurred and the perimeters of the room dissolve into the recesses of a room. Floors, furniture and accent details are good places to start if you are thinking about using black. Use it to introduce rhythm (see page 58) with, for example, black and gilt balusters on a staircase, a heavy ebony picture frame with silver-gilt detailing, a black cane chair or a blackened brick hearth.

Below: Black and white is a perennial favourite of teenagers or anyone who wants to make a strong statement.

Opposite: Don't be scared to use dark colours in the transitional zones of the house, such as a hallway or staircase. You actually notice the contents or furnishings of a room more when set against a darker backdrop.

METALLICS

It is generally thought that metallics are introduced only through light fixtures, furniture, mirror and picture frames or stainless steel appliances. Yet using metallic paint or wallpaper creates a quietly glamorous environment, which is very sophisticated and fashionable. Redolent of the hedonistic exuberance of the 1920s, gold and silver are associated with drama, wealth and power. Equally, it can be simple, understated and quietly bewitching. For a look of restrained sophistication, gold and silver can be mixed together in equal parts to make what I call "gilver," a metallic absolutely suited to the timeless classic scheme.

My gently glittering wallpaper Stardust is a clever way to experiment and enjoy the fascination that sheen adds to a room. There are 28 muted colourways, which, owing to wallpaper's unique texture, can be combined in modern stripes, vertically or horizontally, to create a retro chic room.

Family silver, antiquities, gold bowls or objets d'art, silver- or gold-leafed tables or pieces of Murano glass with a metallic patina are simple and marvellous ways to add a luxurious sheen to your decorating plan.

Opposite: Mildly reflective, the use of metallics is a very glamorous way to spice up an otherwise featureless or ordinary room. I love the sexiness of the brass in this casual shower room.

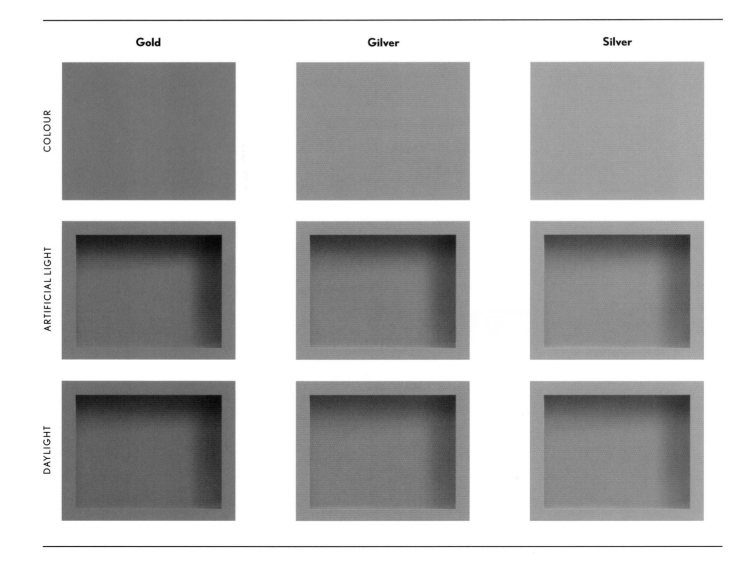

	Gold	Gilver	Silver
COLOUR			
ARTIFICIAL LIGHT			
DAYLIGHT			

Opposite and above: Gold is frequently used on picture frames, but the beautiful metallic sheens can be really appreciated on 3 dimensional objects as well. Look out for contemporary sculptures or accessories in bronze, zinc or steel.

COMBINING COLOURS

While a single colour can have its own identity, rather like a solo musician, a palette is like an ensemble or orchestra. When I approach a new project, I find it helpful to think about planning the colour combinations in terms of composing a piece of music. For example, you might want to create a balanced harmony of neutral tones picked out using a key soloist. And just as musical orchestration often relies on variations of themes – in which a melody is repeated but with its rhythm, harmony or structure changed – so the core and accent colours of a scheme can be chosen to add interest without sacrificing unity. The melody, or the accent colour, creates the atmosphere while the variation, or the core colour, offers definition. I have applied these musical rules to the development of my wallpaper range, aptly named Orchestration.

As with music and musicians, the magic and beauty of colour arise from your own personal interpretation – your unique way of putting the colours together. Combining colours and finding harmonies – as well as having the confidence to express them – are a form of language.

THE COLOUR WHEEL

To understand the different approaches to creating a palette, it helps to look at a colour wheel, which illustrates how the different colours are interrelated. The simplest type of wheel shows only the unadulterated hues (without white or black added). The wheel is divided into coloured segments, one for each hue, arranged in the order in which they appear in the spectrum. Thus the three primary colours (red, yellow, blue), which are the only hues that cannot be created from any other hue, are spaced equally around the circle. In between them are the three secondary colours (orange, green, violet), each of which is made by mixing the two primaries flanking it.

If you then mix each primary with each adjacent secondary colour, the six new colours are the tertiary colours (red-orange, yellow-orange, yellow-green, blue-green, blue-violet, red-violet); some colour wheels include these, too, so that there are twelve segments in all.

When using the colour wheel to plan a colour scheme, remember that only the fully saturated hues are shown. In practice, you are likely to be using tones or shades of at least some of your chosen hues. If you are thinking of using, say, a soft yellow, which is yellow with white added, the segment coloured bright yellow is the one you look at on the wheel.

TYPES OF COLOUR SCHEME

No colour works in isolation, and finding a new combination of colours that look wonderful together can be both rewarding and exciting. Although the sky is the limit when it comes to possible combinations, colour schemes fall into just three general groups: monochromatic, analogous and contrasting.

Opposite: A monochromatic colour scheme uses only tints and/or shades of the one colour and works best in neutral tones.

MONOCHROMATIC SCHEMES

This type of scheme is based on one colour, which is adjusted by adding white to lighten the hue or black to darken it, producing a tint or a shade respectively. A monochromatic colour scheme uses only tints and/or shades of the one colour, theoretically through the whole room. In practice, however, the palette is often augmented with white or another neutral, and is still regarded as monochromatic. I find that this type of scheme works best with neutral colours, yet any monochromatic scheme can be spiced up with interesting materials and textures.

Interiors using this approach tend to be both tranquil and stylish – in fact, a monochromatic scheme is regarded as one of the most chic looks today. It is also perfect for a minimalist décor and provides a fantastic backdrop for displaying fine art. Another good reason for choosing this type of scheme is the ease and flexibility of updating or reviving it.

> Adding pin-pricks of colour to a monochromatic scheme will balance, emphasize and enhance the solo nature of the palette. Always use it more than just once, however – repetition ensures unity.

> Ways of adding to this simple, pared-down environment include introducing a variety of materials such as marble, stone, bare plaster and different colours of wood. A personal favourite is to use a touch of smoked or tinted glass alongside a metallic effect, such as "gilver" (see page 110). This subtly smartens and glamorizes any room.

Right: This monochromatic scheme is not limited to flat surfaces. All the elements of the room are visible and make up the whole composition.

Above: Variation of texture is as important as sheen in the chromatic arrangements of surface and material. Gravel, terracotta, wood and cane all mutate into a pleasing tonal balance in this Mediterranean courtyard garden.

Opposite: The smoky mid-grey of a raw textured wall is chromatically combined with a gun metal desk, a black lamp and waste paper basket, and a stainless steel clock and paper tray in this groovy urban loft.

Above: Unpainted gaps on the painted floor where carpets once lay form a fantastic geometric pattern of monochromatic variations.

Opposite: A simple mirrored candlestick and low painted wall define the monochromatic simplicity of this monastic bedroom.

ANALOGOUS OR RELATED SCHEMES

Any three colours that are adjacent to each other on a twelve-colour wheel can be the basis of an analogous scheme. The middle colour is referred to as the ruling colour. (For example, in a combination of blue-green with blue and blue-violet, the ruling colour is blue.) This type of scheme can also be regarded as having what's called a monochromatic effect – one dominant colour with two additional colours – but it offers more nuances than a monochromatic scheme. Sometimes analogous schemes are called related or harmonious schemes – the harmonious aspect of the related threesome is the fact that this is the combination most often seen in nature. One of the greatest advantages of an analogous colour scheme is that it offers visual unity and a sense of calm. It will be at its most harmonious when the ruling colour is a primary colour, which makes for a smooth visual transition.

> Take care not to overuse the adjacent colours or the effect could become overstimulating or depressing.
> This approach would work well if you used large, bold patterns alongside a similar colour palette of smaller scale.
> As with monochromatic schemes, bringing in different textures is a good way to add interest. My favourites are combining rough with smooth, for example a heavy jute or hessian (burlap) with a soft and pretty silk or a coloured velvet.

Above: The intricate patterned walls in orange, yellow and green in this gorgeous hallway feed through to a citrus yellow kitchen – a fine example of a related colour scheme.
Opposite: Panelled doors are a great place to experiment with related colour schemes. Here the yellow of the panel beds jump onto the walls over grey green stiles and rails.

Left: Patterned wallpaper, dado (wainscot) and the background of these wall motifs feature three different tones of aqua in an inspiring related colour scheme.
Opposite: The use of different textures as well as tones in a harmonious colour scheme creates a restful environment for all.

Above: The related rhythms of yellow-green columns in plaster, fabric and stone in this dramatic hallway is crowned with the large dental work on the cornice (coves).
Opposite: A sludgy boot-green door opens into a sunny limewashed yellow entrance hall creating an inviting related colour scheme decorated with grey green cartographic prints of rural walks and the lie of the land.

Above: Staggered glazed pots and cute painted steps in related colour schemes provide inspiration and relief for an otherwise simple staircase.

Opposite: The sleek green glass floor supports the yellow focal point on a spiral staircase in this contemporary landing.

CONTRASTING SCHEMES

Schemes based on colours that are roughly opposite each other on the colour wheel are called contrasting schemes. One type of contrasting scheme is the complementary scheme, which is based on complementary colours. These are two hues exactly opposite each other on the colour wheel (red and green; yellow and violet; blue and orange; etc). When a complementary pair are placed side by side, the maximum amount of contrast is created and the colours enliven each other, so that they look brighter and more intense than usual. (The reason is that the eye sees one more naturally than the other and then craves a balance.) This creates a strong, dynamic and visually appealing palette.

A variation on the complementary palette is the split-complementary scheme, which combines a hue with the colours adjacent to its complement (such as blue with yellow-orange and red-orange). Yet another type of contrasting palette is the triadic scheme, combining three hues that are the same distance apart on the colour wheel (the three primaries, the three secondaries, or three equidistant tertiaries such as yellow-green, blue-violet and red-orange).

It is worth experimenting with different tones and shades when using a contrasting approach, as it is imperative to understand how the colours work together and it is not easy to visualize or imagine how the palette will work. You will know the winning result when you see it – when the proportions of colour exhibit harmony and equilibrium and are pleasing on the eye. Remember that it is ultimately personal. The decision to combine hues that are mellow or bright, flat or sharp, shows your personality and aesthetic taste.

> If you like the look of contrasting schemes but are afraid they'll be overwhelming, remember that one colour (generally a cool one) should be allowed to dominate. Using equal amounts of each colour would look very unsettling, as they would seem to be fighting for attention. Also, you can give the main colours "breathing space" by using neutrals, light tones, and white around them.

> Don't forget that you most certainly do not have to use the fully saturated hues that appear on the colour wheel – schemes incorporating "softened contrasts" using tints and/or shades of the hues can be much more subtle and easier to live with.

> A lick of paint in a complementary colour around a prized possession can create a show worthy of a museum. And there's no need to limit yourself to paint with this trick. For example, you could draw attention to a central piece of furniture by surrounding it with a rug, or placing it in front of curtains, in its complementary colour. Even an old sofa, say, that you scarcely even notice can be revived in this way, without a bit of reupholstery. After all, the furniture, fixtures and fittings deserve as much importance as the four walls.

> Sometimes there is a colour you simply adore but haven't quite found the courage or an appropriate place to use. Why not paint those surfaces usually hidden from view, such as the inside of your kitchen, linen or laundry cupboards or cutlery drawers? It will make a refreshing change from the nondescript colour that was probably originally used – and certainly will make a difference to the feelings you have about putting things away after use.

Opposite: Sexy contemporary neon lighting mixes the strong contrasting colour
scheme of this indoor swimming pool set for skinny dipping late at night.

Opposite: The rich red fabrics and trimmings of this glorious day bed are the perfect contrast for the marvellous green walls in a traditional spare room.

Above: The pastel pink walls and eau de nil green architrave is a classic example of a restrained contrasting colour scheme that is quietly glamorous.

Above: The quirky scheme of red and green in this Irish cottage is a grand example of how the Irish aren't afraid of use a contrasting colour scheme against all odds with great effect.

Opposite: Areas often hidden from everyday view are a great place to experiment with a contrasting and bolder colour choice. I simply love these colourful attic stairs where I imagine the children might run to hide.

PLANNING & APPLICATION

"It's the wallpaper or me. One of us has to go."

OSCAR WILDE ON HIS DEATHBED

Careful colour planning incorporates not just the flat surfaces but all the room's contents – the patterns, rhythms and variations created by the shapes of everything in the room. The English poet Laurence Binyon, writing about Persian art, said it "depends for its power on that profounder eloquence of related form and colour which affects our minds and emotions in a region deeper than articulate language can reach except in poetry." The same could be said of a well-designed room scheme.

The Russian theatrical director and designer Theodore Komisarjevsky was also aware of the power of colour and form. Describing his conception of a synthetic theatre, he wrote, "Everybody knows that with certain combinations of colours and lines, just as with combinations of sounds and movements, one can achieve a definite psychic effect on the spectator."

SETTING THE SCENE

There is, in fact, an analogy between the setting for a stage performance, utilizing set design, and the setting for everyday life, utilizing interior decoration. Both encounter the same problem. In the theatre, it is to make the decoration a part of the play and not an added distraction. In an interior, it is to make the decoration a part of the ordinary, but no less important, activities and aspirations for which it is a location and background.

Therefore, when collecting paint samples and creating your mood board (see page 52) remember that your final, edited choice of colours should always be governed by the requirements of the room. Ask yourself the following questions:
> Do you want the decoration to be light or dark, gay or sombre, temporary or permanent?
> Are there any colours that have an inherent similarity to, or association with, the architectural shapes in a given interior?
> How may the function of the interior be expressed in terms of colours, lines and shapes in addition to architectural shapes?

Right: I recommend you find yourself a big desk or a dedicated space in which to work and set out all your ideas and planning tools.

COLOUR RELATIONSHIPS

Previously we discussed colour groups individually, which is the best starting point, particularly as a paint chart often consists of an abstract grid of small rectangles representing a colour group. However, because the eye registers a hue by comparing and associating it with other colours, we cannot choose a colour in isolation. We must consider it in the context of what other colours will be in the room. In other words, design involves colour relationships.

In the previous chapter we looked at the three main types of colour relationship:

> Monochromatic (pure relationship incorporating both shade and tone)

> Analogous (involving related, harmonious colours)

> Contrasting (maximum difference using complementary opposites)

Even if you know broadly which of the above types of scheme you'd like to use in a room, narrowing your choice down to a particular scheme can be difficult. Swamped by the multitude of colours to choose from, you may simply feel overwhelmed by an embarrassment of riches. However, the following guidelines should help you combine colours with greater ease.

> You can make any colour the climax of a colour theme by increasing its proportionate size and relative degree of purity.

> A palette consisting of a limited number of colours is usually more comfortable to live with, and therefore more successful, than a complicated variety of colours in the same room.

TONAL VARIATIONS

A lot of us are so fixated on the wall colour that we overlook the skirting boards (baseboards), door frame and doors, panelling, window frames and windows, and other mouldings. Too often I see rooms in which these elements are all painted in one tone of white – which means that it is impossible to create the correct visual balance. Just as an uninterrupted solid colour is seldom effective throughout a traditional house, a single colour from floor to ceiling in a large room rarely produces the best results. By taking the time to appreciate the architectural features, and using careful tonal variations to distinguish them, you can enhance the natural fall of light in a room and avoid that all too sharp, freshly painted look.

> Break up the area by using a variety of similar tones on several wall treatments such as above and below the chair rail, on the skirting board (baseboard) or picture rail, or on the moulding and panelling of the doors and door frame.

> I like to follow a rule from dark to light; here's how you can, too. Think of the tones as 1, 2, 3 and 4, graduating in darkness, with 1 the lightest. Use the palest colour (1) for the ceiling. Paint the flat plane of the skirting board (baseboard) and chair rail in the darkest shade (4), which is slightly darker than the walls (3), and paint their mouldings in (2), which is slightly lighter than the walls. The cornice (cove) and picture rail could be painted with the same lighter colour (2), which is halfway between the wall and ceiling. This creates a crescendo of tone from dark at the bottom to light at the top.

> In addition, the moulding on the cornice (cove) and picture rail could be picked out in a metallic "gilver" (half gold, half silver – see page 110) depending on the degree and level of ornamentation you want.

There are various ways to treat this tonal approach, which depend on the architectural elements of a room and differ in each architectural period. The remainder of this chapter, therefore, looks at the broad principles of Georgian, Regency, Victorian, Edwardian and Modern architectural styles. All of these warrant discussion regarding careful colour planning and application, particularly because of the way in which we like to occupy and redecorate domestic period buildings today. In addition, there is a section on the urban loft, converted from industrial/warehouse buildings, but because relating them to a specific colour arrangement is difficult, they are covered more through the use of innovative materials.

Opposite: Different tones on these picture frames create interest and give visual balance to a simple plain wall.

Opposite: Planning your paint work doesn't need to be limited to one colour on one wall. Think about how you could enhance each wall with elegant painted borders or dados.

Above: Try to think about the overall proportion of floor to ceiling; in this example dark grey is used to only a quarter of the overall height of the room, any higher and the ceiling would start to feel too low.

THE GEORGIAN PERIOD

Often called "the age of elegance," the Georgian period saw the appearance of terraces (rows) of houses arranged around squares, which became a significant feature of British cities and towns. In the grand rows of properties, every effort was made to ensure that as many rooms as possible were lit by windows.

Simple mathematical ratios were used to determine the height of a proposed window in relation to the width and shape of the room, as found in classical architecture. The proportions of each section of a wall – cornice (cove), frieze, picture rail, field, chair rail, dado (wainscot) and skirting board (baseboard) – were specified, as they corresponded to the sections of a classical order, or column. As a result, Georgian exterior and interior architecture is characterized by beautiful proportions and balance.

The decoration of Georgian houses, as with all other eras, was a major indicator of wealth and status in society. For example, elaborate plaster and stuccowork, along with gilding, woodcarvings and paint effects, were expensive and were therefore reserved for grander houses of the merchant classes.

Wallpaper had not been used in wealthy homes until the advent of flock paper, which imitated textiles, at the end of the seventeenth century. Other styles of wallpaper also became fashionable and more widely available, including multicoloured, realistic-looking pictorial scenes that were block-printed, as well as hand-painted "China papers" and imitations of these.

Softwoods became the most economically versatile material to use for the interiors, unlike in previous periods, when oak was generally used for panelling, windows and doors. However, softwoods were less durable than oak and needed to be painted instead of treated, so it was during this period that paint became particularly important. Off-whites, buff-greys and stone colours were frequently used for plaster and softwood-panelled walls. Iron and red oxides were the cheapest pigments during this period and by today's standards were rather dull. It was therefore the murky shades of brown and green that predominated including colours such as Thames Mud and Tarlatan. Alternatively, much more vivid saturated colours, such as Chelsea Green, Chalcedony, Rhubarb pinks and Chinese Emperor were also favoured. Coloured fabrics also played a significant role. Rich coloured silks and velvets were much in vogue, as were crimson, yellow and sage green Indian calicoes.

Today there is a multitude of choice with regard to paint colours but you don't have to follow a historical palette slavishly. I believe colour is so personal that one can have freedom of choice for the walls. However, for all decorative architectural elements it is still imperative to follow the simple rule of light shades beginning at the ceiling and growing darker while moving down to the floor. My paint range of Architectural Colours is a tonal colour by numbers system where each colour has subtle tone differences, from 1 (palest) to 5 (darkest) for use on ceilings, cornices (coves), walls and woodwork. This system can be applied to all architectural styles.

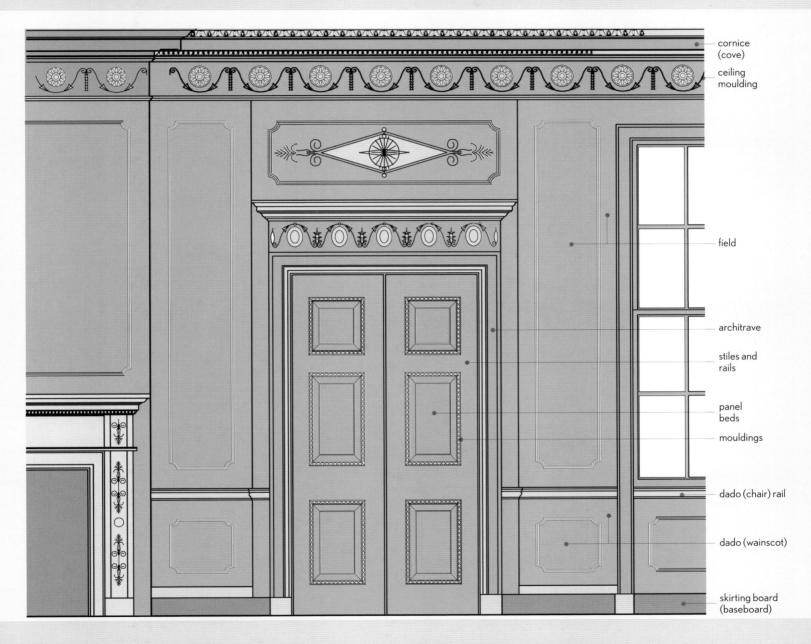

cornice (cove)

ceiling moulding

field

architrave

stiles and rails

panel beds

mouldings

dado (chair) rail

dado (wainscot)

skirting board (baseboard)

Above: A typical Georgian drawing room would include an elaborate doorway, plaster and stuccowork as well as a large window and fireplace - for the purpose of this example we have illustrated these architectural elements altogether. Where there is panelling below a chair rail, I would paint as follows (according to how elaborate the mouldings were): the ceiling in the palest Architectural Colour – No. 1; the cornice (cove) and ceiling mouldings in slightly darker tones Nos. 2 and 3; the picture rail, chair rail and skirting board (baseboard) growing darker in Nos. 3 and 4; and the walls (field and dado, or wainscot i.e., above and below the chair rail) in the darkest tone No. 5. Doors and window shutters could be treated in a similar way: mouldings in No 2, panel beds in No. 3 and stiles and rails in No 4 .

Above: Very grand beadwork and moulding embellished with gold and contrasted with deep teal and rose pink is a fine example of paintwork designed to convey wealth and social status.

Opposite: Three tones of one colour have been used on the moulding in this Georgian room. I like the way the door has been left unpainted to emphasize the doorway..

THE REGENCY PERIOD

The decade 1810–20, when the reigning king, George III, was ill and his son the Prince of Wales (later George IV) acted as Regent, was one of the most transitional periods of English domestic architecture. In fact, Regency style is generally regarded as having lasted several decades. Although designs were still based on the neoclassicism of the Georgian era, the Prince Regent's taste for the exotic had a major influence on architecture and furnishings.

The popularity of Greek architecture (influenced perhaps by the English poet Lord Byron's love of anything Greek) was what most differentiated Regency from the previous Georgian style, creating an architecture of refined elegance and opulence. As with their Georgian counterparts, the typical Regency domestic architecture was stucco-fronted terrace (row) housing, most famously in the grand Regency crescents of British towns.

Architects of the time began to fit window shutters as standard, often using full-length French doors as sources of light. In Regency interiors the architectural model of cornice (cove), field (above the chair rail) and dado, or wainscot (below the chair rail) was still observed but there was now more emphasis on the field. This area lent itself well to strong matt colours such as emerald green, acid yellow, deep pink, crimson and burgundy. Regency colours are perhaps best characterized by their strong and vibrant hues. Flat painted or polychromatic, papered walls and upholstered furniture were often saturated with solid colour or stripes. Lilac and turquoise; deep pinks, marmalade and crimson were striking counterpoints of colour.

Paint treatments included fancy plasterwork, paint or decorative wallpaper. Trompe l'oeil (meaning "trick the eye"), in which three-dimensional effects and optical illusions are created, was particularly fashionable. Trompe l'oeil murals of realistic proportions and scale consisted primarily of designs inspired by scenes from Pompeii but little of this painterly decoration has survived.

Ceilings were often accentuated with motifs and a taste for naturalistic ornament, mainly in the form of a central rose from which the chandelier would hang. Walls and ceilings were sometimes "tented," or draped with silks, brocades or chintzes. Materials such as stone, plaster and marble provided a regal backdrop for all the lavish upholstery and window treatments – rich silks, velvets, taffetas and satins were popular throughout the period. As much of the interior, including the windows, was draped in heavy fabrics, the window frames themselves were kept fairly simple, which makes them perfect today for enhancing your colour scheme without being fussy.

To imitate Regency style, I would suggest the following: contrast strong wall colours with off white woodwork; limit mouldings to grander reception rooms; use bold candy coloured stripes on upholstered furniture or wallpapers to emphasize the symmetry typical of Regency style, and for a finishing touch, the gilt convex mirror is the ubitquitious and evocative Regency artifact to include in any room.

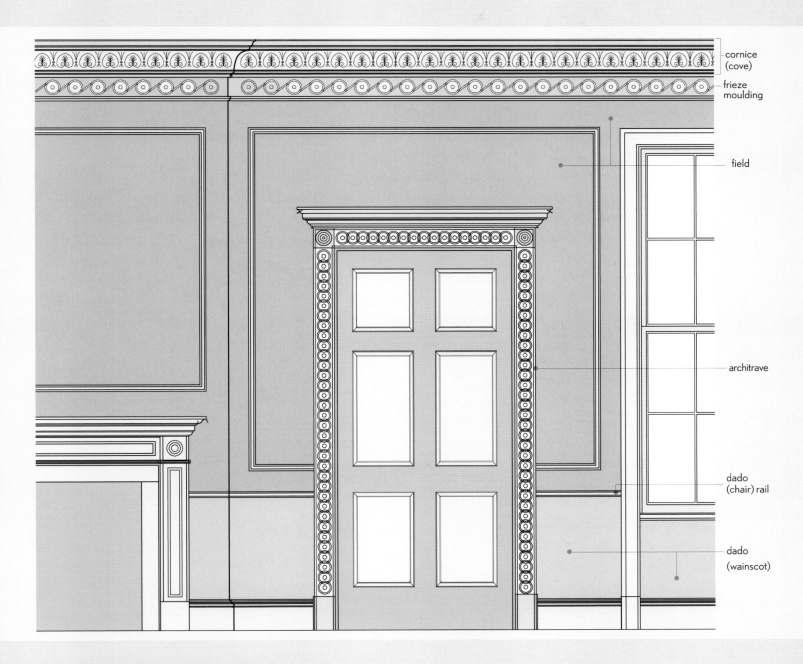

cornice
(cove)

frieze
moulding

field

architrave

dado
(chair) rail

dado
(wainscot)

Above: The Regency period was the last to subscribe to the rules for the division
of walls into cornice (coves), field and dado (wainscot). A correct attention to the
detail could be observed with the cornice (coves) picked out in gold or silver, the
field hung with wallpaper or flat coat of paint and the dado architrave (wainscot)
and moulding picked out in gold or silver.

Above: I like very much the contemporary approach to this Regency library. The cornice (coves) and architrave are all painted in a slightly darker tone of the wall one colour (not white) and the skirting boards (baseboards) and pilasters are painted in an imitation marble to match the fire surround.

Opposite: The conspicuous luxury of this coloured ceiling, silk and fabric loosely based on the colours of Pompeii, is also influenced by contemporary French taste.

THE VICTORIAN PERIOD

The Victorian era (1830–1901) saw a plethora of architectural styles. The two major schools of architecture were neoclassical and Gothic revival, with the resulting "battle of the styles" sometimes characterized as the Greeks vs the Goths.

Victorian housing included the flat-fronted terraced house (row house), the semidetached house and the detached Italianate suburban villa with Tudor-style detailing. With the advent of the railways and development of new manufacturing processes, locally produced building materials became available all over the country. This put an end to all houses in a local area being built from the same materials.

Inside a Victorian house the organization of rooms reflected a clearly defined social order. The public rooms were at the front of the house and were used to entertain guests; these had the greatest amount of moulding and more expensive materials such as marble and slate.

As previously, walls were divided into frieze (from the cornice, or cove, to the picture rail), field (from picture rail to chair rail) and dado, or wainscot (from chair rail to skirting board, or baseboard). Panelling was not used to the same extent as in the previous century but entry halls, libraries, studies and dining rooms did often have exposed wood panelling to provide an impressive backdrop.

Prior to the 1850's, lighter neo classical hues, especially pale pinks, almond, lavender and iridescent whites, remained fashionable, although darker colours such as Very Well Read and Trilogy were used in masculine dining rooms and libraries. These were later overtaken by a stronger palette dominated by traditional, earthy red browns, aniline greens, crisp blues, deep purples and solar yellows. The late nineteenth century witnessed a reaction to this powerful high Victorian colour scheme, and the new decorative style developed lighter more muted colours, which softer yellow ochres, olive greens, rosa reds, pale blue, soft greys and ivory were used to great effect.

It was during this time also that the first rolls of wallpaper were manufactured; previously it had only been available in sheets. Anaglypta and embossed wall coverings were frequently used below the chair rail. Above the chair rail, however, flock and heavily patterned papers grew in popularity, reaching an all-time high in the middle decades of the era. By the end of the Victorian period, the dado (wainscot) was out of fashion for everywhere but the entry hall, stairs and landing, and the picture rail was lower, often level with the top of the doorway.

Ceilings were no longer tented as they had often been in the Regency period, and were replaced with ornate plasterwork on ceilings, ceiling roses and cornices (coves). Elaborate swags, ribs, flowers and festoons allowed the designers to show their talent in grand homes, while in more modest abodes the detailing was much plainer.

My Architectural Colours colour by numbers system can be applied to this style of architecture, as in the example opposite.

cornice (cove)

field

dado (chair) rail

dado (wainscot)

skirting board (baseboard)

Above: In this example of a Victorian drawing room, all the typical architectural elements are illustrated together to demonstrate the different tones of colour in decoration. The personal style of decoration of most people who live in Victorian houses today is less fussy, featuring perhaps a single wall colour rather than a different dado (wainscot), field and frieze. To simplify the choices, the skirting (baseboard) and ceiling could be painted in the following way: ceiling in the palest Architectural Colour No. 1; cornice (cove) and picture rail slightly darker in No. 2; chair rail and skirting (baseboard) growing darker in No. 3; and frieze, field and dado (wainscot) in the darkest tones No. 4 or 5, or both.

Opposite: A contemporary interpretation of the Victorian conventions for elaborate wall treatments, ornamentation and design is shown in this project by Graham Carr.

Above: Inside Victorian houses, the organisation of rooms maintained a clear social order. This parlour has an unlived air as if waiting for a guest of high importance to justify its use.

THE EDWARDIAN PERIOD

The reign of Edward VII (1901–1910) heralded a change in architecture as it followed a period of over-elaboration and dark, cluttered rooms in which the Victorians revelled. The Edwardians were keen to bring light into their homes, and the underlying themes were expensive simplicity, sunshine and air. Detailing was lighter than in the late nineteenth century, looking back to the Georgian era. House frontages tended to be wider so that the entry hall could be of a substantial size. The internal ornamentation was less cluttered and more decorative. It was during this time that people began adopting the modern attitude to one's home, in which it is not so much a status symbol as a refuge from the stresses of daily life. This created a surge in magazines and books on interior decoration. A much more open- plan style of living became fashionable, and dados (wainscots), picture rails and panelling began to disappear. In an Edwardian house today, the one-colour approach would work well.

Edwardian colours were fresher than during the Victorian era: pastel blues, lilacs, leaf green, muted yellows and pearl grey were all typical. The liberal use of fresh flowers in informal arrangements echoed the popular use of floral fabrics and wallpaper. Along with Sheraton, Chippendale, Queen Anne and even Baroque reproduction furniture, wicker and bamboo began to be widely used, adding further delicacy to the style. In the Edwardian colour scheme a strong sense of space in a well lit room was enhanced greatly by white painted ceilings and architectural mouldings. There was a return to a pared down, simpler approach to colour and soft furnishing. Light tones of green in papered or flat painted walls sat comfortably next to related or monochromatic window treatments of the same colour.

A typical Edwardian decoration can be achieved using my colour by numbers system of decorating, as in the example opposite.

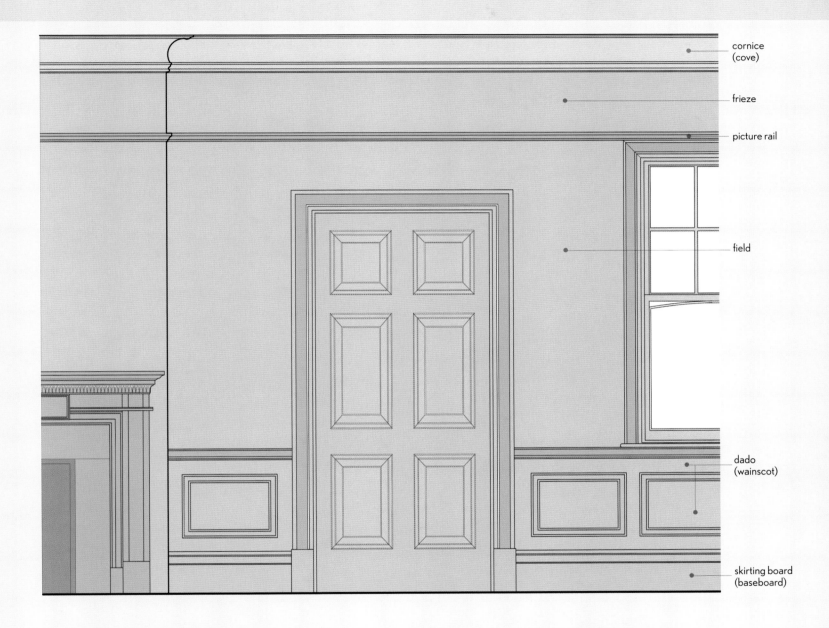

cornice (cove)

frieze

picture rail

field

dado (wainscot)

skirting board (baseboard)

Above: For the purpose of this example all the architectural elements of a typical Edwardian drawing room are illustrated together. The Edwardian house often displayed a mixture of architectural styles. My approach would be to try to unify the choices with any shade of oak to match the enormous number of floor tiles that were produced during this period. Using my Architectural Colours and colour by numbers system, the cornice (coves), picture rail and skirting (baseboard) could be painted in a medium architectural shade No. 2 or 3. The frieze, field and dado (wainscot) in darker shades of No. 4 or 5, and the ceiling in the palest shade, No. I.

Above: Polished oak and hardwoods provide the colours in this neutral room.

Opposite: Very much an example of a pared down and understated return to a simple colour scheme in these contemporary Edwardian first floor reception rooms.

MODERN ARCHITECTURE

The Modern movement, or Modernism, the principal architectural movement of the twentieth century, was a style created by architects and theorists wanting a break from the past and embracing the spirit of the machine age. The main proponents of the movement wanted to change society's attitude, telling people what was good for them. Their aim was to use the newest materials on the market and dispense with ornament, relying instead on the pure architectural form.

The Swiss-born French architect du jour Le Corbusier produced manifestos demonstrating the revolutionary nature of modern architecture. In his *Five points for a New Architecture* he outlined houses on pillars, horizontal windows, free plans, free facades, and flat roofs for sky-level gardens. Most Modernist houses had straight, white outer walls with flat roofs. Globally, this radical architecture was tentatively received, and England particularly viewed the style with suspicion. Even those designers who were committed to the use of concrete used timber, brick and stone as part of the construction and slowly reintroduced the use of colour in the exterior.

The theory behind such a stark approach and lack of detail was that Modernism offered a rational basis for a healthy, hygienic and efficient lifestyle. Architects such as Le Corbusier claimed their style was more honest to its materials, but the overall inspiration was dedicated to an aesthetic delight in space, colour and light which traditional and revival styles couldn't offer. Nearly all domestic architecture during this period was either detached or semi-detached but there was no opportunity for terraces (row houses).

With the elimination of pattern and the use of refined smooth plaster on walls, there was little need for paint and wallpaper. It was only postwar Modernism that introduced a more organic approach, allowing a less rigid scheme with plywood and varnished woods becoming popular.

Modernism turned its back on what was considered unnecessary exterior and interior ornament, such as cornices (coves), friezes and dados (wainscots). The ceiling also lacked any decoration. Fireplaces remain popular architecturally, despite the alternative form of heating available. Understated elegance is achieved with a minimum of decorative distraction. The extensive use of man made new materials such as glass, chrome, steel, linoleum and cork, were complemented by a decorative palette that made minimal use of colour and pattern. This served not only to emphasis the form and texture of architectural fittings and furnishings but also to enhance a general sense of light and space aided by glazing. Many rooms were painted purely white or in monochromatic variations of off white such as slate stone, paper, clay or sand to add reflection. Apart from neutral blacks, and occasional and small splashes of primary colours, other popular hues included pastel buff, greige, choca, mocha, and latte.

architrave

skirting board
(baseboard)

Above: I prefer to add a little more colour to the pure Modernist palette, and would approach the paint specification formula as follows: Using my colour by numbers system, I would use the palest shade No. 1 on the ceiling, a slightly darker No. 2 on the walls, a darker shade No. 3 in eggshell or gloss on doors, an even darker shade No. 4 on skirting (baseboard) shadow lines or window reveals and the darkest shade No. 5 in adjacent rooms or inside cupboards.

Opposite: The understated elegance and simplicity of this modern room is due to the great expanse of space, the use of different materials and the lack of unnecessary interior ornament.
Above: The transparent and reflective sculptural forms of perspex, steel and glass furnishings exploit the modern qualities and demand for new materials in this design-conscious apartment.

THE URBAN LOFT

With the shift in land property prices in major urban areas, much of the commercial industry has moved away from town centres. This has given rise to the conversion of many centrally located commercial and industrial premises as domestic dwellings, and the modern phenomenon of urban loft living. The apartments have been marketed in terms of their architectural distinction, their space, their centrality and the social attributes of city-centre living. Their residents are often professional and managerial workers, many of whom see themselves as pioneers of a new form of city-centre living. The purity of the Modernist movement was already compromised by the over production of tiles and wallpapers and in the urban loft home these have been developed or replaced by interesting textures and the use of real materials – different kinds of stone, exposed brick and glass.

As with the Modern movement, the large scale and lack of domestic architectural details have allowed these previously industrial buildings to be redeveloped so as to incorporate an open-plan way of living. Large open space is once again being explored. Stud walls were added to create private spaces, and this allowed colour to be used in an intriguing way that works perfectly with any of the schemes discussed in the previous chapter. All colours play a pivotal role in the design of the urban loft, often having to lend cohesion to a disparate collection of elements and modern technology. Personal colour choices are established in the urban loft more than any other period, as all boundaries of room and areas of mobility are deconstructed or broken down. A favourite colour can be utilized as vibrant focal point of an interior, either in paint form on walls, in floor coverings, on a signature piece of furniture, or by using coloured lighting.

The redevelopment of huge warehouses has been experimental but offers a fantastic way of expressing a number of diverse schemes all in one place. Although there are no actual "rules," the use of warm textures and subtle soft colours works particularly well with bare brick walls. This type of living can be a challenge but with the help of large furniture pieces and an abundance of personal possessions the space can become cosy and comfortable.

Above: Solid colours or textures on one wall are a simple device to decorate and separate zones or various areas of the open plan loft. Discreet gas operated floating fireplaces also permit both a focus and a distant viewing line for the occupants. Bolder colours or materials can be explored, as all rules are broken... think Andy Warhol's silver foil Factory!

Above, right and opposite: One of the key components of the urban loft or global village design is the marvellous storage solutions required for the way we like to live today. Move in, give it personality and colour and hire a fantastic cleaner would be the key considerations for me in these larger than average spaces.

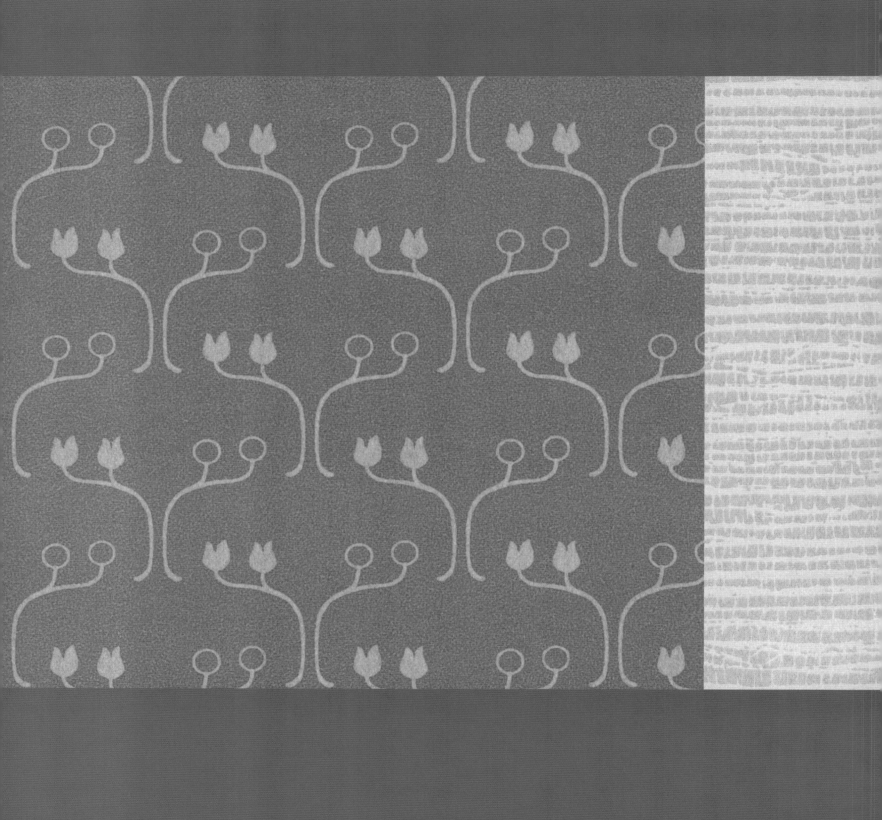

RESULTS

CASE STUDY BADALING, JAPAN

> NATURAL TONES AND TEXTURES

Untreated bamboo is the main visible building material in this villa overlooking the Great Wall of China. Designed by the Japanese architect Kengo Kuma using local materials, the villa is in complete harmony with its environment. From the outside it blends unobtrusively into the landscape and from the inside appears to merge seamlessly with its surroundings. Windows and glass walls look out onto the traditional elements of Chinese paintings – mountains, rocks, water and bamboo – as well as the fantastic view of the Great Wall.

Bamboo-clad ceilings are combined with closely spaced vertical bamboo canes that throw decorative light patterns across the interior spaces and furnishings. By filtering the light and air, the delicate bamboo partitions mean that the interior subtly reflects changes in the weather and landscape, while glass walls flood the space with light.

A greenish-black slate floor runs through the villa and out onto the veranda, creating continuity between the rooms and further linking the interior and exterior. It also contrasts dramatically with the white walls and with the strongly textured bamboo surfaces. In a similar vein, the bathrooms are lined with black marble, punctuated by the colours of glass and ceramic as well as bamboo.

Furnishings in soft, neutral tones such as dove grey sofas, white-covered beds and tatami mats on the floors echo the tones of the bamboo and the pale gravel gardens outside, and help to maximize the impression of lightness and simplicity. Small tables display calligraphy brushes, china bowls, spices and flowers, referencing the traditional colours and flavours of the location.

With its minimalist lines, natural materials and neutral colours, this villa fosters an atmosphere that is peaceful and meditative. Almost monastic in its simplicity, the monochromatic colour palette and understated design are quietly confident and respectful of the spectacular views, amalgamating modern and traditional Asian with striking clarity and focus.

Top: The importance of the house's location was a serious consideration when designing this bamboo Chinese villa.
Above: The rhythm of the bamboo clad ceiling and closely spaced vertical canes throw decorative shadows across the interior furnishings.
Opposite: Floor to ceiling glass windows look out onto traditional elements of a typical Chinese painting; mountains, rocks, water and bamboo.

Opposite, above and above top: Furnishings were kept deliberately soft and neutral. Dove-coloured grey sofas, covered beds, tatami mats, and greenish-black slate floors echo the tones of the bamboo and the pale gravel paths immediately outside.

Left: The rustic charm of the entrance hall belies the deliciously weathered textures of each room throughout the house.
Opposite: Original wall decorations, painted on canvas, were revealed after layer upon layer was removed during the sensitive restoration process.

regular intervals to give the impression of a patterned carpet. The panels, dado (wainscot) and high double doors were painted light grey, while the plaster ceiling and coving are whitewashed and delightfully chalky in texture.

The top-floor rooms are simply decorated. Above the pearl grey dado (wainscot) the walls are painted a soft yellow, pink, green or blue, depending on the colour of the tiled faience stove in the room. The stove, which was used for heating, was one of the most important features in a Gustavian room. Usually the starting point of a colour scheme, the stove was often tiled in Chinese-inspired blues and in white.

Curtains were hung in double rows either in a single colour to harmonize or contrast with the colours of the walls and furnishing fabrics, or white with accoutrements in related shades.

Throughout the house, the delicate colour scheme is predominately an analogous palette of harmonious pale tones. The effect, enhanced by the tiled stoves, crystal chandeliers, neoclassical furnishings, beguiling floral or gingham textiles and simple, gilt-kissed neoclassical ornamentation, was of restrained elegance throughout. Today the beautiful patina of the timeworn surfaces evokes all the chaste majesty of the Gustavian period.

Ekensberg's regal splendour is underpinned by a modest palette, and its success lies in its understatement rather than overemphasis – the modest rather than the pretentious. As with other Gustavian buildings, it is these quintessentially Swedish qualities that make this house so very comfortable and desirable.

CASE STUDY LAKE MÄLAREN, SWEDEN

ORIGINAL GUSTAVIAN PAINTWORK

One of the most charming aspects of Ekensberg, a 1790 villa outside Stockholm, is the worn and dilapidated texture of the original paintwork on the walls, woodwork and flooring. Restored by Lars and Ursula Sjoberg, the original Gustavian wall decoration, painted on canvas in 1795, was revealed after layer upon layer of wallpaper and newspaper had been removed.

The broad floorboards, of spruce and pine, were originally painted in shades of golden brown and chocolate to imitate light oak parquet laid in a lozenge pattern, while other floors have been stencilled with red and green stars or petals at

Above: Undressed window treatments allow maximum light to flood into the main rooms and underpins the modest approach to the furnishing of this Swedish house.

Opposite: Harmonious fabric colours were chosen to complement the tones and texture of the time-worn surfaces of the wallpapers and woodwork.

Opposite: A tile faience stove was an important feature in a Gustavian room. This was often the starting point for a colour scheme using Chinese inspired blues and white.

Above: The eye is always attracted to where the eye and hand has rested before such as the doors on this bedroom stand.

Above: Chinese-red lacquered front doors symbolize good luck, success and joy at the entrance to this Beijing designer's home.
Opposite: Sleek green leather sofas balance the lashings of red lacquered woodwork painted throughout the framework and original window bars of the house.

CASE STUDY BEIJING, CHINA

JEWEL COLOURS

Driven by her love for all things Oriental, Belgian-born jewellery designer Jehanne de Biolley has revitalized this Beijing house, incorporating copious amounts of traditional red lacquer woodwork and green leather accents. In the drawing room of the large north pavilion, the smart geometric window bars, door frames and internal pillars are all painted a beautiful rich red, of an intensity that takes many coats to achieve. When contrasted with sleek green leather seating, the result is beautiful and striking, echoing the colours of the precious and semiprecious stones she uses in her jewellery. A colour scheme of complementary opposites such as this one requires careful consideration of all proportions to achieve a pleasing balance, and so the room's high ceilings are a great advantage visually.

Offsetting the strong contrast of the red and green, the walls are a neutral grey tone made by mixing black ink and white plaster. Also in this shade is the varnished grey concrete flooring, mottled and cracked by humidity as if made up of irregular paving slabs. A collection of blue and white china of many periods provides a satisfying mixture of old and new, while old carved woodwork, claret-coloured leather trunks and Oriental artefacts add personal touches that resonate with meaning and memory.

The varnished green slate bathroom is the perfect sanctuary, allowing the eye to rest after the rich Chinese shot silks and glossy columns of the adjacent rooms. Outside, in a cobbled courtyard, the colour scheme continues in the fresh green foliage of pine, walnut, pomegranate and bamboo growing beside glorious red lacquered doors, gates and woodwork. In China red symbolizes good luck, success and the expression of joy, which is very apt for the joyous colour scheme of this home. It must be truly magical in winter when the courtyard is covered in freshly fallen snow.

Above: Claret-coloured leather trunks and Oriental artefacts add personal
touches on smart geometric bookshelves that resonate with meaning and memory.
Opposite: High ceilings and low lateral seating work their visual advantages to
create the correct proportions of colour and light.

Above: The varnished green grey slate bathroom is a cool neutral retreat that allows the eye to rest after the glossy red columns of the adjacent rooms.

Opposite: Black lacquered Chinese screens, beds, chairs and cabinets provide a satisfying mix of old and new in the bedroom.

CASE STUDY NORMANDY, FRANCE

A BOLD AND DRAMATIC PALETTE

Intense colours are one of the distinguishing characteristics of Andrew Allfree's eighteenth-century French château. Vivid colours provide a dramatic backdrop for a beautiful collection of furniture, artefacts and fabrics. The success of the boldly contrasting palette lies in its direct relationship with the dramatic scale and proportions of each room. Colours are sourced from different countries and periods and are used according to compatibility of scale, form and ornamentation, rather than specific style or date.

In the main entrance hall the walls are tromp l'oeil woodgrain. Chinese red lacquer cupboards anchor each of the four corners of the room, which opens onto the quaint outbuildings and black Welsh mountain sheep that populate the pastoral landscape surrounding the château.

A pair of white urns sits in the window of a west wing office, where the walls are painted brown and the woodwork below is painted tractor green. Shelves are lined with French and English antique books chosen more for their handsome styling and coloration than their content. A red velvet curtain thrown over a Regency sofa is a rich foil for bright blue walls and an Italian painting. This is a room where one could snooze after lunch, dreaming of previous sojourns abroad.

A visit to Sicily inspired the paint scheme in the dining room with its pronounced wooden columns which contrast with, and counterbalance, lava-coloured walls and pale grey woodwork. An 1830s English chandelier hangs above a Regency table and antique mahogany chairs with red leather seats. Quirky focal points include a statue of Hypnos and a wooden carving centred on a mirror. A hot pink Indian fabric and the château's mirrored boiserie fireplace backdrop the Salon Indien with its host of disparate styles including blue Murano chandeliers, Genoese white marble console, and a Roman granite vase. Quaint outbuildings and black Welsh mountain sheep populate the pastoral environs.

The result is a luxurious triumph and superb example of how a contrasting colour scheme can be used to dramatic and sumptuous effect in a large country house.

Top: Ceilings are painted in the same wall colours so as not to distract from the contents of each room.
Above: Bold contrasts of colour work well with the dramatic scale and proportions of the rooms in the château.
Opposite: An English chandelier and white marble urns punctuate the cool, dark interiors like meteorites floating in their own atmosphere.

Opposite: Moulding and architrave all painted the same colour in the Green Salon contrasts with blue and silver damask banquette and red upholstered gilt wood chairs.

Above: The eclectic collection of old and new furniture (adorned with a dead fish) deliberately adds to the surreal cinematic styling in this vivid solar yellow room.

Above: Luxurious fringed canopies lined in blue-green silk contrast with rust-red upholstered armchairs and bedspreads, sit comfortably against dark indigo walls.

Opposite: A red velvet curtain is thrown over a regency sofa as a rich foil for the vivid blue walls and Italian landscape painting of classical ruins.

Left: Metallic convex wall tiles in kitsch bubble shapes morph and reflect the circular living room.
Opposite: Accents are restricted to retro chic chairs and dark blue glass vases. This is spot-lit by circular skylights, allowing the sunlight to flood in.

CASE STUDY SYDNEY, AUSTRALIA

COOL CONTRASTS

A contrasting retro chic colour scheme embodies the spirit of this über-cool summerhouse in Sydney. The choice of colours is controlled and marshalled into cool lapis lazuli blues and gritty Concorde greys on the walls, floors and ceilings, with burnt orange velvet and blood-red or rust-coloured leather upholstery on the furniture.

Situated on a precipice, the summerhouse plunges and levels out from a spectacular rock face typical of the local area. The cantilevered sandstone rock face projects right into the interior, making a striking feature as it steps a steady course through the entrance hall, past the start of a cascade of spiral steps and out onto the glossy black roof terrace teeming with southern hemisphere colour and light.

Circular skylights in the living room ceiling flood rings of daylight onto the polished concrete floor like spotlights on a stage. Textural interest is also very important here as mirrored convex wall tiles morph reflections of the room into kitsch futuristic bubbles to form pretty evanescent patterns around the room. In the bedroom, glass bricks form an outsized headboard while serving as a room divider between the sleeping area and an en suite sanctuary and deep blue ablution zone.

The glass floor-to-ceiling windows around the edge of the summerhouse reveal the marvellous vista of eucalyptus and banksias running right up to the house. This wall of vegetation forms a spectacular corona underneath an arched ceiling punched with the circular skylights, like a piece of Swiss cheese.

This groovy house and colour scheme echo Sydney itself – a city noted for the colours of its beautiful rock formations and waterways and a place where the sea, sky and sand are just a loose foothold away.

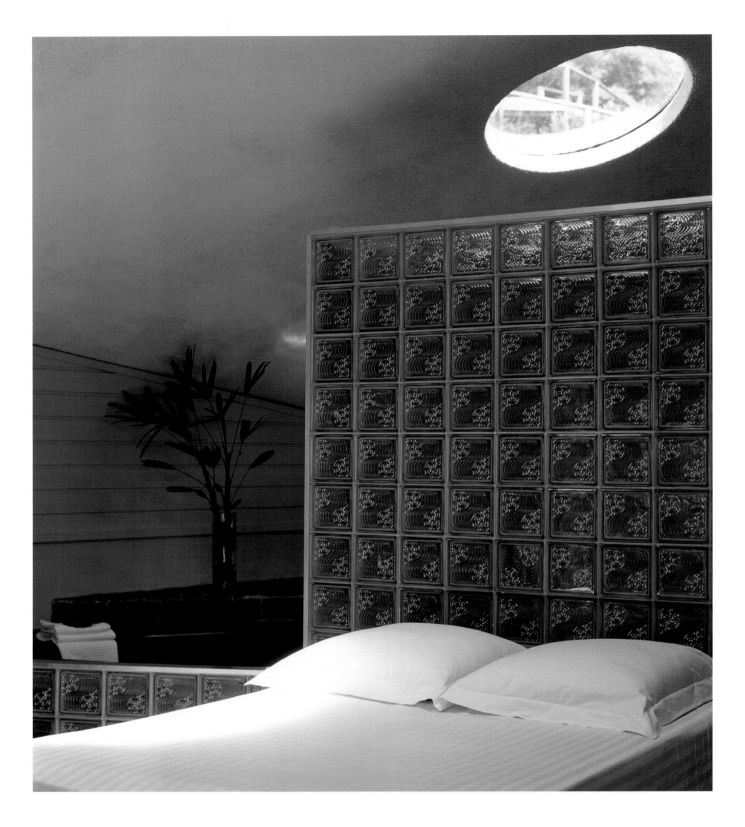

Above: A glass brick wall separates the basic bedroom from the adjacent bathroom to form a robust semi-transparent partition – a homage to modern materials.

Opposite: The house is built around a large sandstone overhanging rock face creating a fine example of primitive-luxe.

Left and opposite: Appealing to the design conscious, the colours of your house can now be controlled simultaneously with electronic distortion. This ubiquitous all-white staircase and kitchen can be constantly redesigned with ever-changing coloured lighting (see overleaf).

CASE STUDY LONDON, UK

SWITCHED-ON COLOURS

Advances in technology mean that lighting, once a traditional and fairly predictable aspect of interior decoration, offers innovative new ways to alter a colour scheme. Domestic lighting is now capable of generating a variety of colours to suit every mood or time of day. Washes of computer-controlled lighting across the surfaces of a room can simulate an infinite variety of colour nuances that are difficult to distinguish from "real" colour. For example, in this London apartment an all-white staircase can take on a vividly contrasting colour scheme at a moment's notice.

The use of computer-based technologies to programme colour "landscapes" reaches beyond the simple colour changes previously achieved only with paint. The new lighting techniques can alter the colours of furnishings, accessories and other details to redefine a space within the home. Striking and impressive in its visual display, this so-called spectacle lighting facilitates shapes and colours that create an infinite number of images in our brains, challenging our spatial perceptions and injecting our daily lives with new visual pleasures. From the subtlest to the most extreme, a great parade of chromatic tonalities can be reproduced and programmed.

Virtual decoration characterizes our age, because so much of everyday life is increasingly dominated by visual images. The age of the computer and electronic imaging presents a profound shift in the status of the home and the way we engage and decorate it today.

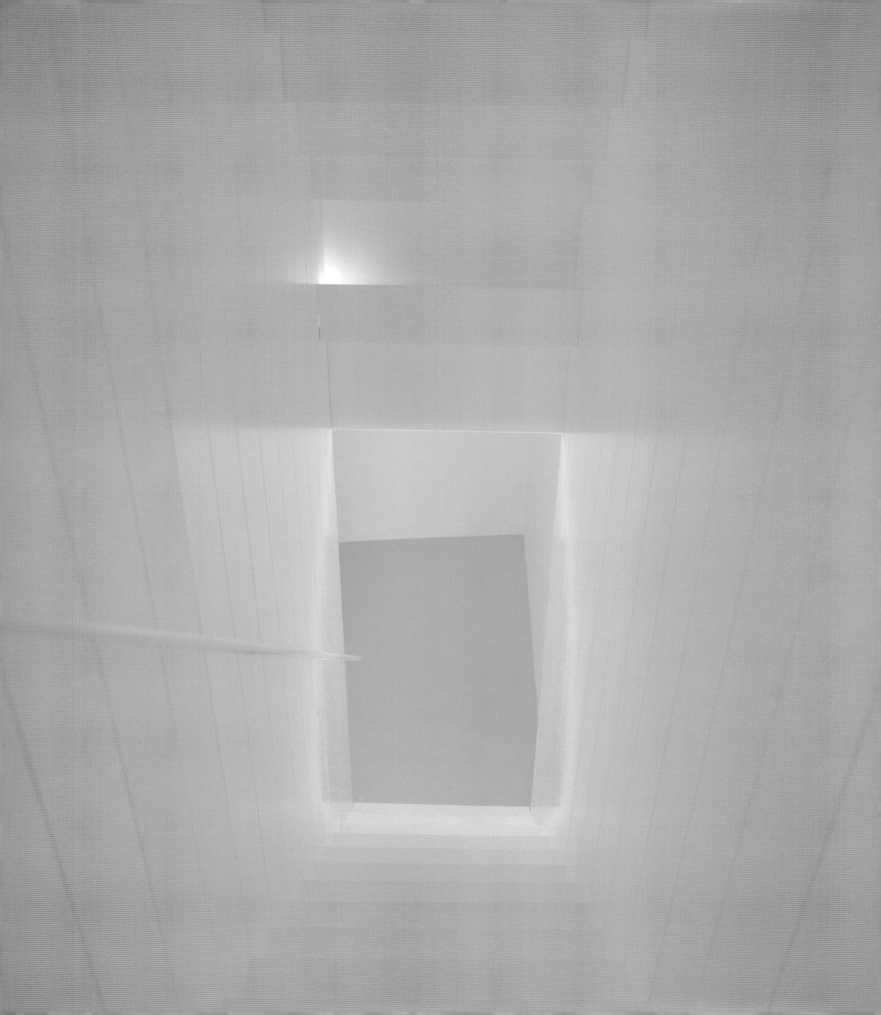

Above: All the woodwork window frames and doors are painted in the same vivid emerald green.
Opposite: Like following a piece of string in Venice so you don't get lost, the singular placement of one particular green is comforting and familiar.

CASE STUDY ANCONA, ITALY

HIGH-IMPACT MONOCHROME

Restricting a vivid colour to a relatively small area, such as a door, rather than a large area like an entire wall, makes it seem more vibrant. This is because bright colours are so stimulating to the eye that they can be visually tiring when used over a large surface. Emerald green, which has always been a favourite of mine, can be particularly effective when painted on the smaller details of any interior. For the same reason, green is ideal for exterior railings, trellis, doors, woodwork and room dividers.

I often say that colours can put homes in order, and that is certainly the case at Casa McQueen, a restored Italian farmhouse, where the placement of one particular green is perfect. The same shade has been applied throughout the whole house on doors, shutters, window frames and skirting boards (baseboards) and, most attractively, in one or two thin lines at eye level in every room. The effect is to lead the occupants through a maze of simply decorated, monochromatic rooms as if following a ribbon. At the same time, the green woodwork marks the boundaries of each room and defines the living area.

All the rooms are simply decorated and monochromatic, with floors of bare stone, terracotta or wooden floorboards. The farmhouse has been renovated using original and reclaimed materials wherever possible, in order to retain its traditional atmosphere. Stripped wooden tables, rush-seated chairs, freestanding cupboards and wrought-iron beds sit neatly under exposed oak beams. Throughout the house the marvellous emerald green and white décor is punctuated only by the occasional informal bunch of flowers, earthenware vases, simple lights and objects.

The consistency of this accentuated colour scheme creates a sense of calm, restfulness and balance while at the same time adding luminosity and cheerfulness to the interiors. The decoration has become an integral part of the architecture, and its success lies in its visual purity as well as its function. It is a very simply conceived colour scheme that is simultaneously delicate and strong, fine and brilliant.

Opposite and above: The monastic simplicity of this use of singular colour as a navigational and decorative design tool transmits a consistent and calm feeling.

Left: Understair cupboards are painted in a vibrant shade which creates elements of surprise and delight for young and old.

Opposite: A series of rooms alternate in terms of decorative devices rather than colour. A painted room leads to a papered room and so on.

kitchen and utility cupboards, wardrobes and other hidden areas that are accessed regularly are painted in a delicious hot rhubarb pink. This injects an element of surprise as if to reveal the subconscious of the house without affecting the overall mood and style of the room.

Colours and textures modulate between painted and papered rooms like instruments playing an orchestral score. In the study a glossy green plastic desk sits at right angles to a wall painted in a squid-ink blue-black shade. In the adjacent hallway, black and white biomorphic lithographs by Alexander Calder hang side by side on a clean-lined geometric wallpaper.

An uncluttered kitchen/dining room is practical and fashionable with the minimum of fuss. Simple and functional, an upholstered, mirrored banquette is a mixture of analogous colours – green, brown and china blue – while a low, modular, black walnut bench alongside adds graphic impact.

The pale and interesting blonde colour schemes in the bedrooms are soft and easy to awake to every day. Here, basic whites, creams and beiges have been mixed on fabrics and furnishings to add interest to a monochromatic colour scheme.

In every room of this London town house, a range of textures has been used to add depth and interest to complement the colour palette. The result is a decorative scheme that suits the sophisticated mixture of pared-down modern with classic shapes and patterns, creating an effect of understated comfort and a perfect poise.

CASE STUDY LONDON, UK

SOPHISTICATED UNDERSTATEMENT

The modern classic look of this London town house is enhanced with a predominantly neutral, monochromatic scheme, while the neat proportions and elegant architecture of the house create ideal opportunities to use splashes of strong colour in niches and alcoves or as accessories. Quietly glamorous, the decorating scheme caters for both masculine and feminine tastes, providing an ideal compromise for a home in which the occupants have different tastes or the space is multifunctional.

For versatility and comfort, as well as visual contrast, the colours used here are employed on two or three levels without losing the flavour of the other core colours. The interiors of

Above: A fusion of glass, furniture and stone adds textural interest and an injection of coloured accents to the natural greige sitting room.

Middle: A sliding pear wood and fixed wallpapered panel cleverly disguises a disused fireplace and bookshelves either side.

Opposite: A study room that was used only at night has been painted dark squid ink blue to blur the boundaries making the room feel infinite.

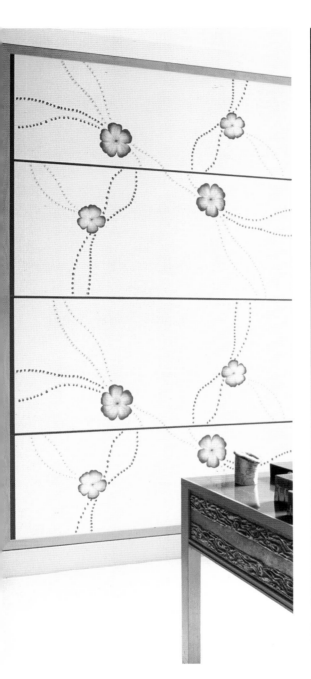

Opposite: A mirrored slip was inserted above and below the upholstered banquette to light and modify the sight lines of this static built-in piece of furniture.

Above: Pearlescent pale grey kitchen cupboards with a bold splash of colour on the insides makes a refreshing change and is a great way to add your favourite colour.

Above: Soft duchesse satin curtains, glass beads and screen printed Roman blinds
are mixed together to create a monochromatic colour scheme of soft white and cream.
Opposite: A fresh pale and interesting blonde colour scheme in the bedroom
can be especially easy on the eye to awake to every morning.

CASE STUDY CAPE COD, USA

POSTMODERN MONOCHROME

Garagia Rotunda, a late twentieth-century postmodern masterpiece by the American architect Charles Jencks, embraces architectural traditions through its allusions to the past. Sited on Cape Cod, Massachusetts, the house mixes classical and vernacular elements such as blue posts, beams and split pediments.

The entrance gate is painted in ten shades of blue, capturing the ever changing blues of the sky, ocean and ponds. Light blue roof beams lead the eye to balconies, which project out into an undisturbed landscape of hog cranberry, bayberry, witch grass, scrub oak and pine. Architectural shadows form geometric patterns in tonal variations of the Grecian blue across the blue and white tiled studio floors. The monochromatic use of colour in the building's bone structure is extraordinary: at times a beam or post appears to evaporate into the blue background of the Cape Cod sky. At such moments the sky becomes part of the composition.

The colour red is used only twice – at one end of the studio to indicate the electricity meter and at the other end to draw attention to the sky. Structural elements are syncopated or set in counterpoint to create a colourful concord of harmonious internal parts.

The furniture, constructed from 10 x 10cm (4 x 4in) timber studs, is also painted in various blues to distinguish major and minor components. Textiles incorporate the same proportions of this colour as the stud wall, visually merging the hard and soft furnishings. A table and chairs, painted in different shades of blue, echo the rhythm of the studs.

In the same colour scheme, an aedicule, in the shape of a classical temple with quoins, stores personal possessions. Its permanently billowing curtain, created by a bent metal clothes hanger, is Jenck's tongue-in-cheek symbol for the architectural winds of change that flow through the monochromatic palette of Garagia Rotunda.

Above: Ten different shades of blue were used to paint this fabulous studio.
Opposite: Architectural shadows form ever-changing patterns and variations across blue and white tiled floors in front of an aedicule in the shape of a classical temple.

RESOURCES

GLOSSARY

A

Accent colours: A colour used in small quantities to lift or to add punch to a colour scheme.

Achromatic: No hue present.

Achromatic simultaneous contrast: Simultaneous contrast that works with the interactions of black, white and greys.

Additive colour mixing: Creating colour by adding light to a dark background.

After-image: A reaction that happens when the brain supplies the opposite or complementary hue after the observer stares at a particular hue.

Analogous colour scheme: Colour scheme based on three or more hues that are located next to one another on the colour wheel.

Analogous hues: Hues that are adjacent to one another on the colour wheel. Also known as related hues.

Aniline dye: The first synthetic dye, based on coal-tar and alcohol derivatives.

Arbitrary colour: The effect of colour that an artist produces after imposing feelings on an object's colour. This abandons natural colour.

Architectural order: A series with the lightest value at the top and the darkest at the bottom.

Artificial light: Light that is created by artificial means. Types include incandescent and fluorescent.

Asymmetrical balance: Balance that relies on non-symmetrical design components in which the two sides of the work are not the same.

B

Balance: The total appearance of the work that shows unity. It can be symmetrical or asymmetrical.

Bezold effect: An effect that happens when colours are changed through putting them together with other colours. Also known as the spreading effect.

Binder: A vehicle in which pigments are converted into a workable tool.

Broken hue: A colour that combines all primary colours but in unequal proportions.

Broken tint: Colour made from black or white being added to a broken hue. Known as natural grey.

C

Cast shadow: A shadow thrown by an object onto a nearby surface.

Chiaroscuro: Distribution of shadows and light in painting.

Chroma: The saturation or purity of a colour.

Chromatic: With a hue.

Chromatic black: Black resulting from mixing red, yellow and blue.

Chromatic greys: Greys resulting from mixing white with a chromatic black.

Chromaticity: A measure of the combination of saturation and hue of a particular colour.

Chromatic simultaneous contrast: Simultaneous contrast that works with colour/hue changes resulting from surrounding colours/hues.

Chromotherapy: Using colour for healing purposes.

Colour blindness: Imperfect colour vision that results in inaccurate identification of colours.

Colour harmonies: Colour schemes that are harmonious.

Colour schemes: Combinations of pure hues and their variations.

Colour theory: A study of colour that explains colour interactions and reactions by order, observation, scientific facts and psychology.

Colour wheel: A circle showing colour relationships.

Coloured grey: Result from adding a pure hue's exact value of grey.

Complement: See Complementary hues.

Complementary colour scheme: A type of contrasting colour scheme using complementary hues.

Complementary hues: Hues that are directly opposite one another on the colour wheel.

Cones: Cells in the retina that are used to see colour in bright light.

Contrast: Visual difference of colours.

Contrasting colour scheme: Colour scheme using hues that are roughly opposite each other on the colour wheel.

Cool greys: Result of mixing white with a commercially produced black.

Cool hues: Hues that are related to blues. They include: yellow-green, green, blue-green, blue, blue-violet and violet. The coolest hue is blue-green.

Core colours: The dominant colour of a chosen colour scheme that creates definition in a room.

Core of shadow: Most concentrated area of darkness on an object.

D

Diffraction: The break-up of a beam of light into light and dark bands or coloured spectra, after striking an object.

Dimension: Four properties of colour: hue, value, intensity and temperature.

Disappearing boundaries: The effect achieved when hues of the same or near values that are adjacent to each other on the colour wheel are used side by side.

Discord: The effect achieved when the value of a hue is opposite its natural order.

Dissolving boundaries: The effect achieved when analogous broken hues of equal value are used side by side.

Double complementary colour scheme: A colour scheme based on two sets of complementary hues.

Dye: Pigment dissolved in a fluid.

E

Emphasis: Creation of visually important areas on which the viewer can focus.

F

Flat colour: One solid area of colour used as a design element.

Fluorescent light: A type of artificial light produced by electric current passing through a gas-filled tube, causing the gas to emit radiation which reacts with a phosphor coating in the tube, creating a glow.

Focal point: An area in a composition or room that gives emphasis so the viewer will be drawn to it.

Form: A three-dimensional shape that implies volume.

Fovea: The area at the back of the retina where cone cells are contained. This is the area of the sharpest colour definition.

G

Gesso: A primer that provides a consistent painting surface.

Glazing: Layering of transparent colours.

H

Harmonious colour scheme: Another name for an analogous colour scheme, based on three or more hues next to each other on the colour wheel.

Harmony: The visual accord of all parts of a design, resulting in unity of the whole work.

Highlight: The lightest value on the surface of an object.

Hue: The name of a colour, indicating which wavelength appears to be predominant.

I

Incandescent light: A type of artificial light produced by electric current passing through a filament. Types include tungsten, halogen and low-voltage halogen.

Intensity: The strength or saturation of a hue.

Intensity scale: The arrangement of colour chips in order of intensity.

Interaction: The way a colour reacts to its placement or position.

Interference of light: The reaction of colour caused by a change in the viewer's position.

Intermediate hue: See secondary colour.

Interpentration: An interaction between colours that occurs along the edges of touching colours.

Intervalled scale: A colour scale that shows a smooth visual transition from one component to the next.

Iridescence: A luminous effect that comes from the way colours play when viewed from different angles.

Irradiation: Contrasts that are formed between an object and the background.

K

Kinetic effect: The effect that results from a warm/cool contrast.

L

Lake: A combination of a pigment and a dye to extend the pigment range.

Light notations: Notations assigned by Goethe to hues, indicating their strength.

Light wheel: A colour wheel arrangement of hues that are the result of projected coloured lights. Its primaries are red, blue and green, and this is the basis for additive colour.

Line: A continuous mark on a surface, which shows motion and contour to images.

Linear composition: Clean delineation of forms.

Local colour: The effect of colour in clear daylight.

Logical shading: Shading that is seen when there is no definite light source.

Lost and found contour: The effect of shapes and forms as they melt or integrate with the background.

Luminance: A measure of the value of a mixture of lights.

Luminosity: The glowing impression given off by a colour.

M

Middle-value grey: A visibly equal mixture of black and white.

Midtone: The colour resulting from adding grey to a hue.
Monochromatic colour scheme:

The use of a single hue and its variations to convey colour to a composition.

N

Natural order: Using a black background and moving from grey then to white, or using a white background and progressing from grey into black.

Natural pigments: Pigments that are taken from animal, vegetable and mineral substances.

Negative after-image: An after-image that is seen as a complementary colour of the viewed colour area.

Neutral: Strictly speaking, a colour, such as black, white or grey, that does not contain any pure hue. Also often used more loosely, to mean colours such as tan, sand and cream.

O

Optical light: The effect of colour seen in any condition other than white daylight, such as candlelight, sunrise, sunset or rain.

P

Pantone Matching System (PMS): A system based on nine colours, along with white and black, which shows what percentage one needs of each to produce a particular colour.

Partitive colour: Placing colours side by side to create different reactions.

Pastels: Soft, pale discords of hues.

Primary colour: A pure hue that cannot be obtained by mixing. Mixing primary colours forms other hues and colours. The primary colours of pigment are red, yellow and blue (used in subtractive colour mixing); the primary colours of light are red, green and blue (used in additive colour mixing).

Progression: The repeating of a design element in an orderly format that allows changes of rhythm to create a sense of motion.

Proportion: The relationship formed between one part of a design or mass and another part, one part and the whole piece, and all the parts to each other and the whole.

Pure hue: A hue that contains no

black, white, grey or complementary colour in its formula.

Q

Quaternary colour: A colour resulting from mixing a primary colour and a tertiary colour in visually equal proportions.

Quinary colour: A colour resulting from mixing a secondary colour and a tertiary colour in visually equal proportions.

R

Reflected light: Light bounced back from nearby surfaces.

Refraction: The bending of a ray of light when it enters a prism or different material.

Related colour scheme: Another name for an analogous colour scheme, based on three or more hues next to each other on the colour wheel.

Repetition: The sequence of design elements within a composition.

Rhythm: A dynamic design principle that creates unity using various forms of repetition.

Ruling colour: The middle hue in an analogous colour scheme.

S

Saturation: The relative purity of a colour.

Secondary colour: A colour resulting from mixing two primary colours in visually equal proportions.

Shade: The colour resulting from adding black to a hue.

Softened contrasts: Tones of contrasting hues. Contrasting colour schemes can replace some or all of the pure hues with these.

Split complementary colour scheme: A type of contrasting colour scheme combining a hue with the colours adjacent to its complementary hue on the colour wheel.

Subtractive colour mixing: Creating colour by using pigments or dyes to absorb light.

Surface colour: The hue that most closely describes the colour of an

image or parts of an image.
Symmetrical balance: Balance that relies on a "mirror image" of design components, in which both sides of the work are equal.

T

Temperature: The "warmth" or "coolness" of a colour.

Tertiary colour: A colour resulting from mixing a primary colour with a secondary colour adjacent to it on the colour wheel, in visually equal proportions.

Texture: The relative smoothness or roughness of a surface.

Tint: The colour resulting from adding white to a hue.

Tone: A tint, midtone or shade of a hue, dependent upon how much white, grey or black has been added to it. Also sometimes used to mean midtone or simply "colour."

Translucent: Denotes that light can pass through the material partially; semi-transparent.

Transparent: Denotes that light can pass through the material so that the object behind can be seen distinctly.

Triadic colour scheme: A type of contrasting colour scheme using three hues that are equidistant on the colour wheel.

V

Value: The lightness or darkness of a colour.

W

Warm greys: Greys that result from mixing white with a black that has been produced by mixing red, yellow and blue together.

Wavelength: A measure of light: the distance between crests in a wave of energy. Different wavelengths of light are perceived as different colours.

INDEX

The publishers would like to thanks the following sources for their kind permission to reproduce the photographs and illustrations in this book.

2 Luxproductions.com; 4-5 Alan Weintraub/arcaid.co.uk (Architect: Agustin Hernandez); 6 Simon Upton/The Interior Archive (Designer: Lars Sjoeberg); 8 Christopher Simon-Sykes/The Interior Archive (Designer: Julian Bannerman); 9 Simon Upton/The Interior Archive (Designer: Albert Hadley); 13 Luke White/The Interior Archive (Designer: Chiara Dona/Donatus); 14-15 Adrian Dennis/epa/Corbis; 17 Simon Upton/The Interior Archive (Designer: Andrew Allfree); 20-21 Herbert Ypma/The Interior Archive; 23 Simon Upton/The Interior Archive (Architect: Lubetkin); 24 left Andreas von Einsiedel (Designer: Fiona Adamczeswki); 24 right Simon Upton/The Interior Archive (Owner: Ilse Crawford); 25 Simon Upton/The Interior Archive (Designer: Christopher Leach); 26 Richard Bryant/arcaid.co.uk (Architects: Sergio Puente & Ada Dewes); 27 Simon Upton/The Interior Archive (Property: La Colombe d'Or); 28 Simon Upton/The Interior Archive (Designer: Matthew Smythe); 29 Mark Luscombe-Whyte/The Interior Archive (Designer: Muriel Brandolini); 30 top Simon Upton/The Interior Archive (Property: Chatsworth); 30 bottom Andreas von Einsiedel (Designer: Frank Faulkner); 31 Simon Upton/The Interior Archive (Designer: Jehanne de Biolley); 33 bottom Ianthe Ruthven; 33 top Henry Wilson/Redcover.com; 34 left & right Herbert Ypma/The Interior Archive; 35 © The Joseph and Anni Albers Foundation/VG Bild-Kunst, Bonn and DACS, London 2007 - Albright-Knox Art Gallery/Corbis; 37 © Kate Rothko Prizel & Christopher Rothko ARS, NY and DACS, London 2007 - Christie's Images/Corbis; 38-39 © ADAGP, Paris and DACS, London 2007 - Vincent West/Reuters/Corbis; 40-41 Miro Kuzmanovic/Reuters/Corbis; 42 Gérard Degeorge/Corbis; 44 top and bottom Mark Luscombe-Whyte/The Interior Archive (Designer: Jose de Yturbe); 45 © Barragan Foundation/2007, DACS - Herbert Ypma/The Interior Archive; 47 Freyda Miller/Corbis; 46 Ray Main/Mainstreamimages/David Garland; 48 Natalie Tepper/arcaid.co.uk; 53 Luke White/The Interior Archive (Designer: Chiara Dona/Donatus); 54 Fritz von der Schulenburg/The Interior Archive (Property: Charlottenhof/Schinckel); 57 Chris Tubbs/Redcover.com; 59 top © ARS, NY and DACS, London 2007 - Richard Bryant/arcaid.co.uk; 59 bottom left Martin Jones/arcaid.co.uk (Architect: Frank Lloyd Wright) ; 59 bottom right Richard Bryant/arcaid.co.uk (Architect: Frank Lloyd Wright) ; 60 & 61 Simon Upton/The Interior Archive (Property: Chatsworth); 62 Simon Upton/The Interior Archive (Designer: Thierry Despont); 63 Herbert Ypma/The Interior Archive; 65 Mark Luscombe-Whyte/The Interior Archive (Designer: Muriel Brandolini); 68-69 Simon Upton/The Interior Archive (Designer: Andrew Allfree); 70 and 72-73 Herbert Ypma/The Interior Archive (Architect: Jose de Yturbe); 75 Ken Hayden/Redcover.com; 76 Christopher Simon-Sykes/The Interior Archive (Property: Calke Abbey); 77 Ken Hayden/Redcover.com; 79 Dan Duchars/Redcover.com; 80-81 Christopher Simon Sykes/The Interior Archive (Property: Marston Hall); 82 Henry Wilson/Redcover.com; 84-85 Grant Govier/Redcover.com; 87 Fritz von der Schulenburg (Property: Roman Baths/Schinckel); 88 Simon Upton/The Interior Archive (Architect: Annabelle Selldorf); 89 Simon Upton/The Interior Archive (Property: La Colombe d'Or); 90 Premium/arcaid.co.uk; 92 Simon Upton/The Interior Archive (Property: La Colombe d'Or); 93 Simon Upton/The Interior Archive (Oddili, London); 95 Simon Upton/The Interior Archive (Designer: Andrew Allfree); 96 Simon Upton/The Interior Archive (Designer: Vanessa Branson); 97 Simon Upton/The Interior Archive (Designer: Lars Sjoeberg); 98 Simon Upton/The Interior Archive (Owner: Vanessa Branson); 100 Mark Luscombe-Whyte/The Interior Archive (Property: Casa Legorreta, Mexico); 101 Fritz von der Schulenburg/The Interior Archive (Property: Roman Baths/Schinckel); 103 Simon Upton/The Interior Archive (Designer: Andrew Allfree); 104 Christopher Simon-Sykes/The Interior Archive (Property: Eastnor Castle); 105 Herbert Ypma/The Interior Archive (Architect: Juan Sordo Madaleno); 107 Simon Upton/The Interior Archive (Designer: Fabien Frynz); 108 Chris Tubbs/Redcover.com; 109 Simon Upton/The Interior Archive (Designer: Andrew Allfree); 111 Simon Upton/The Interior Archive (Designer: Roberto Gerosa); 112 Mark Luscombe-Whyte/The Interior Archive (Designer: Frederic Mechiche); 113 Simon Upton/The Interior Archive (Designer: Alison Spear); 114 Judd Foundation. Licensed by VAGA, New York/DACS, London. Photo credit: Rainer Judd, Courtesy of Zing Magazine; 116 to 117 Ken Hayen/Redcover.com (Architect: John Pawson); 118 Andreas von Einsiedel (Designers: Holger and Marion Stewen); 119 Dan Duchars/Redcover.com; 120 David George/Redcover.com; 121 Winfried Heinze/Redcover.com, 122 Henry Wilson/Redcover.com; 123 Di Lewis/Redcover.com; 124 Christopher Simon Sykes/The Interior Archive (Designer: Julian Bannerman); 125 Simon Upton/The Interior Archive (Designer: James Andrew); 126 Ken Hayden/Redcover.com; 127 and 128 Simon McBride/Redcover.com; 129 Ken Hayden/Redcover.com; 131 Klaus Frahm, Hamburg; 132 David George/Redcover.com; 133 Richard Bryant/arcaid.co.uk (Architect: Schinckel); 134 Ianthe Ruthven; 135 Robin Matthews/Redcover.com; 138-139 Judd Foundation. Licensed by VAGA, New York/DACS, London. Photo credit: Rainer Judd, Courtesy of Zing Magazine; 141 Simon Upton/The Interior Archive (Property: Carlyle House); 142 Fritz von der Schulenburg/The Interior Archive (Property: Roman Baths/Schinckel); 143 Winfried Heinze/Redcover.com; 146 Fritz von der Schulenburg/The Interior Archive (Property: Charlottenhof/Schinckel); 147 NTPL/Andreas von Einsiedel; 150 NTPL/Andreas von Einsiedel; 151 NTPL/James Mortimer; 154 Simon Upton/The Interior Archive (Designer: Graham Carr); 155 NTPL/Michael Boys; 158 NTPL/Geoffrey Frosh; 159 Ken Hayden/Redcover.com (Designer: Nye Basham); 162 Alan Weintraub/arcaid.co.uk (Interior. Richard Neutra); 163 Simon Upton/The Interior Archive (Designer: Tiffany Dubin); 166 left Simon Upton/The Interior Archive (Designer: Alex Shaw - The Penthouse); 166-167 Marcus Wilson-Smith/Redcover.com; 167 right Ray Main/Mainstreamimages (Design: Paul Priestman); 170-173 Simon Upton/The Interior Archive (Designer: Kengo Kuma); 174-179 Simon Upton/The Interior Archive (Designer: Lars Sjoeberg); 180-185 Simon Upton/The Interior Archive (Designer: Jehanne de Biolley); 186-191 Simon Upton/The Interior Archive (Designer: Andrew Allfree); 192-195 Richard Powers/arcaid.co.uk; 196-199 Jefferson Smith/arcblue.com; 200-203 left Paul Raeside/Mainstreamimages; 203 right Ray Main/Mainstreamimages/David Garland; 204-211 Bill Batten/The Interior Archive (Designer: David Oliver); 212-215 Charles Jencks.

Author's acknowledgements
First & foremost this book would not have been possible without the help and support of Sophie Rose Oliver, Louise Chidgey and my agent Arabella Stein in getting me from A to B, which was certainly no minimal task. I am also indebted to Emily Hedges for her picture research contribution, Lucy Gowans who created the artwork and design structure for this project and the staff of Conran Octopus - particularily the skill and enthusiasm of Lorraine Dickey for making this title happen, as well as Sybella Marlow and Jonathan Christie for their patience, advice and guidance. I am also extremely grateful to Georgina Grattan-Bellew and Anthony Little whose inspired ideas, fabulous taste, belief and encouragement set the Paint Library and Architectural Colours in motion, respectively. I would also like to thank all the past and present staff of Paint & Paper Library and in particular, Louisa Mahony, Lucia Huntington, Annabelle Shmith, the Fenty sisters: Brigitta and Julie, Antonia Shand, Mannerings and Agent Townsend, Dr Caroline Skidmore, Beverley Hills Collins, Joao Kimanga, Robert Tandoh and Bubble for all their incredible assistance and support back at the ranch.